Gamify Your Dog Training

Training Games for Group Instruction

Terry Ryan

Illustrations by Jackie McCowen-Rose

Dogwise™ Publishing

Wenatchee, Washington U.S.A.

Gamify Your Dog Training
Training Games for Group Instruction
Terry Ryan

Dogwise Publishing
A Division of Direct Book Service, Inc.
403 South Mission Street, Wenatchee, Washington 98801
1-509-663-9115, 1-800-776-2665
www.dogwisepublishing.com / info@dogwisepublishing.com

Illustrations by Jackie McCowen-Rose
Additional art on page iii and 19 by Carol Byrnes
Dedication page art by Nicolas Bishop

Graphic Design: Lindsay Peternell

Library of Congress Cataloging-in-Publication Data
available upon request

ISBN: 978-1-61781-204-0

Printed in the U.S.A.

More praise for *Gamify Your Dog Training*

When I think of Dogs and Games and making training fun for the dogs, owners and onlookers, I always think of Terry Ryan. Playing games with your dog is the best way to engage your dog's attention and as such, the quickest and certainly, the most enjoyable way to train. Dogs quickly learn that training is fun and that fun has rules. My favorites of Terry's games have always been Dogzilla for sheer exuberance, Dueling Dogs for lightning fast control and Musical Chairs for rock-solid down stays. Read Terry Ryan's *Gamify Your Dog Training* and your dog will be forever grateful. Game on!

Dr. Ian Dunbar, Founder, Association of Professional Dog Trainers

Dedication

For Brody, the dog who made us laugh.

Table of Contents

Introduction

I've remained active in the evolving field of dog training continuously since the 1960s. Much of that time has been spent in the role of classroom instructor. I sometimes wonder why I've stayed with it for so many years. Part of the answer is that I've been having fun. I'm interested in trying new ideas in curriculum development, then checking with the experts, the dogs themselves, on how it's working. I've been influenced by emerging research and also by the success of practitioners I respect. My path has been guided by my own experience working with dogs and their people around the world.

This book is about relationship, communication and having fun while successfully and efficiently training dogs. My emphasis in this book is on playing games in groups. Others have done a fine job of presenting games and exercises for home-alone dogs, one-on-one interactions and games for a more focused, specialty goal. I have additional games with slightly different goals published in my book, *Coaching People to Train Their Dogs.*

Games People Play…To Train Their Dogs was a booklet I wrote in 1996 based on some of the exercises I was using in my pet dog manners classes. It's been out of print for quite some time. It was quickly followed by a sequel, *Life Beyond Block Heeling.* This book, *Gamify Your Dog Training,* contains some of the exercises from those early booklets. More than 60 percent of this book consists of games and activities I have not previously published. Some of the originally published games have been dropped as I have developed better games to replace them. I have personally played or conducted each exercise listed in this book in our local classes and in seminars and workshops throughout the world in such far-flung places as Australia, Brazil, Canada, China, England, Germany, Italy, Japan, Mexico, the Netherlands, New Zealand, Norway, South Korea, Spain, Taiwan, and more. It seems to me that playing with dogs can be the common denominator to help people understand that we're not all that different from one another.

How this book is organized

I'm not sure I properly met the challenge of categorizing the games in this book. The games are meant to provide an opportunity to enhance behavioral skills such as self-confidence in everyday environments. Some of the situations will prove novel, but non-threatening, to the participants. The games are not meant to deal with issues such as reactivity. Rather, the games are meant to increase the fluency of behavior and training skills already in place at a beginner's level. The dogs should have at least some expertise at cued behaviors such as attention, sit, down, come and walking nicely on leash. Most of the games can be cross-referenced many different ways. A glance at the description section for each game will give you a quick hint of what the game is about.

The first section of the book, entitled Setting the Stage for Success, is, in my opinion, the keystone for all that follows. Please read through it thoroughly and you will better understand what the games are meant to accomplish and how to efficiently lead them. Next, look at the headings under each game to determine if it will be appropriate for your particular players. The headings for each game may vary, but will include some or all of the following:

- **Prerequisites and benefits.** This provides a reminder that some behavior and training expertise is recommended. How the game will provide practice for the benefit of the dogs and people is explained.

- **Set-up.** Pre-event planning issues and equipment needed to implement the game are presented. If needed, an explanation of how to organize the playing area (placement of start and finish lines, for example) is mentioned here.

- **Description.** An overview of how the game is played is presented here. You might find this section the most helpful when deciding if the game is appropriate for your use.

- **Game variations.** In some instances, comments on how to vary the game, particularly how to change the game to make it more or less challenging, appear here.

- **A coachable moment.** Value added—this section suggests opportunities for supplemental comments or a quick auxiliary lesson beneficial to the learning experience.

Setting the Stage for Success

Both humans and dogs are social animals. We enjoy each other's company. Games can be a natural extension of the good times dogs and people can have together in a group setting. Training classes, neighborhood barbecues, holiday parties and doggy play-dates are all good excuses for people and dogs to play games. Games provide the often under-served aspect of mental and physical exercise for people and dogs.

Gamify or *Gamification* are the buzz words for a popular trend in adult education. Dog training classes fall under adult education even though we seem to be (somewhat wrongly) concentrating on the dogs. Too serious-minded to "play games"? Okay. Just replace the word "game" with the phrase "training exercise" and we will still be on the same page. It works to think of this book as a curriculum development resource—including some strategies for effective instruction—with a heavy dose of games thrown in! For decades I have used games in each level of my training classes to provide opportunities to practice the basic core behaviors through fun. My goal is to create a learning environment of minimal stress and reduce the possibility of inter-student competition at a time best spent on improving personal bests for each individual couple.

Definitions and categories

For simplicity, my explanations will refer to all dog/human duos as couples, partners or pairs. The human of each couple will be "she" and the canine partner will be "he." If the participants are divided into groups containing multiple pairs, those groups are known as teams. The overall leader of the event will be called the Game Leader (GL) and the designated helpers are called Assistant Game Leaders (AGL).

"Leash work" and "walking with your dog" are used generically. There are a variety of definitions in the world of dog training such as "heeling" or "loose-leash walking." I am avoiding those terms here. It's up to the GL to inform the players, depending on the particular game, what the criteria are for walking their dog on leash. Will the dog be required to stay very close to his person's leg or will he be allowed more room to move about? In all cases, the expectation is for the dog not to pull on the leash.

Who are the players?

Most of the games in this book are designed for groups of self-confident adolescent to adult dogs. They are designed to practice and build fluency on already-learned behaviors. Puppies under 14 weeks of age should not be included in the general game-playing group. Separate puppy events  can be provided for them. Games for young puppies should focus more on introducing new experiences while maintaining a puppy's self-confidence. In carefully monitored situations, and with a dose of common sense, many of the games listed here can be adapted for groups of puppies.

Reactive or fearful dogs won't be in the best position to learn in a general group situation. Create a separate games opportunity for these dogs, directed by a knowledgeable Game Leader and assistants. Even more attention needs to be paid to preserving each dog's personal space, including eye contact from other dogs. Choose games providing a low chance of arousal. Identifying and monitoring arousal triggers and thresholds is important when working with reactive or fearful dogs. When in doubt, space and barriers are your best friends.

If you plan to use these games in your regular training classes, you already have a good idea of the aptitude and, more importantly, the temperament of the dogs and people who will participate. If you find yourself the GL of a group you don't know well, take extra care in your selection of appropriate games. Read carefully the description under each game to determine if it's appropriate for your players. Rather than guess or hope for the best, play some simple, do-no-harm diagnostic games first to help you profile the participants. I've included a few among the first games listed in The Games section of the book. During the initial "get to know you" games, watch for the precursors to inappropriate arousal levels. Again, space and/or barriers are a prudent idea. See pages 13 and 14 for information about interpreting canine body language. Watch for lack of attentiveness and appropriate handling of dogs by their people. Do you perceive red flags? Keep an eye on those couples, assign an AGL to be nearby, and be careful about choosing appropriate games.

Beginners, intermediate or advanced?

Are the games for beginners, intermediate or advanced play-
ers? I have specifically stayed away from labeling games in this
way. There are too many independent variables in each game
to specify the whole as beginners, intermediate or advanced in
skill level. For example, a dog might be capable of the training exercise, but is not appropriate socially or emotionally for a
group situation. A dog might be great at all core behaviors and
many advanced skills. He might be operant and have terrific communication with his
person, however, never having been taught to fetch on cue, this dog would be a rank
beginner at retrieving games.

With creativity, a difficult game can be made easier. Conversely, an "easy" game can be
made more complex for dogs up to the challenge. Some ideas for modifying games are
given in the individual listings.

Specific training techniques and methods

Most of the games here are appropriate for building
fluency with already-known behaviors in novel envi-
ronments. Therefore the widely varying art, science
and mechanics for establishing new behaviors are not
specifically addressed in this book. Personally, I prefer
the use of appropriately delivered positive reinforcement and rely heavily on audible markers rather than
coercion. (An audible marker is a succinct sound, often
provided by a hand-held clicker, which pinpoints the
behavior that will be positively reinforced, usually with
a food treat.) That preference will probably be obvious
to you as you read on.

If you don't know the training method inclinations of your group, make your expectations known in regard to equipment and interactions at your event. You may want to
advise against retractable leashes in class. Have extra equipment on hand should you
find it appropriate to loan different gear. If you will be using or referring to clickers,
everyone should understand or at least be monitored on the proper use of a clicker.
This is best done by a demonstration or interactive drill without dogs. Some examples
appear at the end of this book. If you would rather people not use lures, tell them
your reason why, or perhaps put a limit of one lure or "jump start" per game. Try not
to be a bully or a training snob. Get your point across without causing hard feelings.
You could replace your temptation to say "don't" or "no" with "let's try" or "have you
thought about" or "a good alternative might be."

On-the-spot training

It's up to the GL to determine if extra time will be spent training behaviors involved in each game. It doesn't take much time to help participants break down an exercise so they can succeed at the task or at least a part of the task. In this way the event can lean more toward "can we help you?" instead of "show us what you've got." See examples under the "A Coachable Moment" headings in the various games.

Praise, play and toys as training rewards

Give guidelines on what play interactions are safe and effective in groups. If a game with a squeaky toy is used as a reward for one couple, will it create undo distractions for others close by? What about the effect on others of loud, raucous praise? I don't allow playing with balls at my events, unless the balls have handles or are knotted into a sock to prevent them from rolling away, possibly creating a problem between dogs.

Food as reinforcement

Tell participants that too many rich treats during the event might upset their dogs' stomachs! Treats should be soft so they can be eaten quickly, helping the games run smoothly. Most important, they need to be non-crumble or there will be a minefield of crumbs, attracting every dog in the place. Talk to the participants about an intermittent schedule of reinforcement.

Job descriptions for your staff

Games can be the best thing ever to happen to your group, or the worst. Success boils down to how you, the Game Leader, will plan, explain, supervise and coach the proceedings. The GL's attention needs to be on the participants at all times, not on setting up equipment, keeping score, taking videos, supervising her own dogs, or making coffee. Organize some Assistant Game Leaders (one or more may be needed depending on the nature of the game) to perform any tasks that might take your attention away from the participants. Recruit people known to have good dog and people skills rather than inviting unknown volunteers from the sidelines to help you. At your pre-event meeting, give your AGLs clear job descriptions. An assistant, in her enthusiasm to help or explain, can distract participants from listening to directions from the GL. Ask the AGL to be your extra set of ears, eyes and hands. If you are talking, the AGL should not be. AGLs should discreetly report to you situations that concern them. However an AGL should use her own common sense and intervene immediately if a dangerous situation is imminent. Otherwise, an AGL's role is to quietly, with as little interruption as possible, support you, the Game Leader.

Other AGL tasks might include:

- Listen to the GL's instructions to the participants as the event unfolds. The GL might need to change her plan on the fly. Help carry out the new plan.

- Encourage the event's participants to listen to the Game Leader.

- Help maintain appropriate spacing between participants.

- Help players remember instructions and be ready when it's their turn.

- Set up and tear down between games while the GL explains the next game.

- Set up and/or pass out props if any are required for the game.

- Help keep track of various timing aspects of the games session.

- Know how to use and adjust the sound system if one is in use.

- Play music, if any is planned for a game. Be clear on which music is meant for which game.

- Keep an eye on the spectators. Help them enjoy themselves without interrupting the progress of the event.

Preparing the venue for games

If playing outdoors, leashes and/or a fenced area are a must. Do you have permission to use the space? In public areas can you keep passersby feeling welcome and safe by roping off the games area? I've used bamboo gardening stakes with bandanas tied to the tops for this purpose. Colorful balls of giant, fluffy yarn are lighter in weight and easier to work with than rope. Plastic surveyor's tape is another option. And it goes without saying that you should have insurance coverage as well.

Be aware of the need to provide adequate personal space for each couple, including staging areas. Start and finish lines as well as place markers will be important for traffic control. Cones, stakes, tape, chalk, Post-its and index cards are some of the options depending on if you have an indoor or outdoor venue. On blacktop or concrete, you can draw the lines with white or colored chalk sticks found in a toy store. On dirt or lawn you can use the powdered chalk used on athletic fields. Duct tape adheres to all but the dirtiest or wettest of outdoor concrete surfaces. If you are tempted to use inverted-nozzle landscaper's spray paint, test a small area first to see if it really does wash off. Portable plastic zig-zag play pen sections are versatile and good to have on hand. Slippery floors can be an issue indoors. Use mats, or play games that don't require agility or speed. Reasonably priced interlocking rubber matting squares are easy to set up. They come in a variety of colors. You can organize the colors to help you indicate place-keeping markers or start and finish lines.

Your voice is easily lost when playing games outdoors. Try standing with the wall of a building, a bank of earth or a line of trees behind the players as you face them. This helps to contain your voice. Games can be noisy. Indoor locations can have poor acoustics. People giving cues, dogs panting and vocalizing, praise, cheering...there might be times when it would be helpful if you had a portable microphone with speakers. A headset or pin mic is the best choice. Check the system out ahead of time for feedback screeching, which often depends upon where you are standing.

Equipment and props

Make sure your playing venue has the usual assortment of basic needs. Clean-up supplies are a must. Drinking water and a few bowls are handy, but folks will (should?) probably bring their own. Paper bowls might be good for people concerned about communicable disease. Timing devices (have a back up!), some clipboards, paper and pens should be on hand. Remember to have a charged cell phone handy. Program it with emergency numbers. Know where the first aid kit is located and share that information with the AGLs. Know where to put your hands on extra collars or harnesses and leashes quickly. You might want to provide extra dog treats in case someone runs out. I usually rely on packaged treats kept in the original wrappers so people know what they are giving their dogs. I always have a couple of medium-sized life-like fake (toy) dogs on hand for demonstrations rather than relying on real dogs. Toy dogs that can stand, but can also be formed into a sit are the best. Have them on leashes!

Check all of your equipment and props to be sure they're sturdy, non-toxic and have no sharp edges. Are there any objects small enough to swallow? Remove or flag extraneous equipment that can be tripped over or run into. Be sure to check the area from a small dog's point of view as well as the human's.

The big three

More than any other equipment, Game Leaders rely most on:

Tape. Tape is the most user-friendly, error-free way to indicate start and stop lines, out of bounds, direction of travel and more at an indoor venue. Vinyl floor marking tape is the best because it's specifically designed for floors. Painter's masking tape also works. Both are easier to remove and less damaging to surfaces than traditional duct tape. Think of how the widths and colors of the tape you acquire can be helpful in making your set-up clear to the participants. An alternative is a couple of packs of Post-its. The kind that is 90 percent sticky instead of the other way around will more reliably stay in place.

Cones. These can be used as start and ending markers, visual markers to help preserve personal space between dogs, or to show where spectators can safely view the games. They also make good sign holders. Plastic cones (miniature versions of those the road crews use) can be purchased at sporting goods stores. Beware of the ones with openings in the sides. They knock over easily. I had one incident where a dog got his leg

stuck in the opening. Soccer dots (slightly conical plastic discs) are a lot shorter, therefore more difficult to see, but can serve the purpose. They have the advantage of being almost impossible to knock or blow over. An added benefit is that dogs are not as eager to try to retrieve them. They're also sold at sporting goods stores.

Cards. Decks of regular playing cards can be used as place markers on tape lines to show exactly where on the line you want each couple to stand. They can be used to  break a tie—highest number drawn wins. They can be a means of choosing teams (see page 11). Some of the game descriptions require cards as props for specific uses. Blank index cards serve some of the same purposes. Many games here require prepared-in-advance exercise cards as described next.

Exercise cards

Some of the games ask the dogs to perform a task drawn at random. The tasks are prepared and printed out ahead of time by the GL. Helpful are printer-friendly sheets perforated so that you can tear them into card-sized pieces. A package of blank index cards can be written on by hand. You could print out the tasks on regular paper and insert into envelopes.

Some games might require exercises reflecting different skill and/or complexity levels. You can use differently colored cards to code the exercises. It's up to you to create tasks specific to your chosen game and suitable for the level of your participants. You will probably need exercise cards for at least three or four times the number of players in your class.

Here are a few examples of tasks to print on cards, but be creative and dream up your own exercises. Review the cards before the event to be sure to have the associated props on hand.

- Put an elastic bandage around your dog's belly.
- Ask your dog to lie down while you shake the GL's hand.
- An AGL holds the leash as you walk away five paces and cue sit.
- Dog sits and stays while you sing Happy Birthday.
- Walk together around the cone and back.
- Wipe all four of your dog's feet with a towel.
- Dog sits while you take your shoe off and put it back on.
- Find the closest tree (chair, trash can) circle left around it.
- Ask your dog to lie down and stay as you walk a circle around him.
- Ask your dog to sit, starting from a down position.
- Dog stands totally still (four on the floor), as you pat his head.
- Dog sits while you pull an oversized shirt on and off of yourself.
- Dog sits still while you brush three strokes from head to tail.
- JOKER—Show your dog's favorite trick.

Organizing the masses

How many times have we heard someone say "He's friendly" or "He just wants to say hi"? A dog's tolerance of the proximity of others can change from second to second. Not every player will be able to determine accurately the comfort level of their own dog or that of other dogs. Plan ahead for adequate space, separation between players and traffic control.

A big step toward achieving that is to divide the participants into smaller, more manageable groups. Here are a few strategies for designating sub-groups, referred to as teams.

Some games lend themselves nicely to dividing by the size of the dogs—a big dog team and a small dog team. Counting off is another age-old method of forming teams. Each person in turn declares "one," "two," "one," "two." The ones are a team and the twos are the other team. You can make as many teams as you want this way, but it's fraught with problems. Unless people are in one straight row and paying attention, it soon gets mixed up. I've resorted to walking down the line, making eye contact with a person, politely pointing to them calling out "one" and "two" myself, using one finger or two fingers when pointing. Nowadays I prefer to use a deck of regular playing cards for the task. I'll go through the deck ahead of time to have the same number of cards as participants. I'll make sure there are equal numbers of red and black cards. Holding the deck face down, I'll ask each person to pull a card. You now have a red team and a black team. They can identify each other by holding up their cards and moving into their respective groups. If you want to be fancy, you can prepare a deck of blank index cards in the proper quantity using different stickers to designate each team. It's okay if the teams end up unequal in number if you're playing "everybody-is-a-winner" games. If you do need equal teams, someone can go twice. I stay away from having participants "choose up sides."

One of the main reasons for dividing a large group is to reduce the waiting time for each couple to take their turn. Standing around with nothing to do is never a great idea with a group of people and dogs. You can organize your area to play the same game in different locations, each team with its own Assistant Game Leader as facilitator. If you prefer, you can play two or more different games simultaneously, each team with its own AGL. In games with little equipment to set up, it might be easier for the AGL to do the moving and the teams to stay put.

Demonstrations and your dog

Often the most efficient use of time is to demonstrate as well as explain a game. Have an AGL use a toy dog as her partner rather than a real dog. It's nearly impossible for an AGL to keep her mind off her own dog and on her assistant game leader responsibilities so its probably best for staff to leave their own dogs at home. Why tease the dogs if they won't be able to get in on the action? Keep in mind that borrowing a player's dog to demo sometimes makes the dog uneasy. Read the dog. If you give him back without doing the demo, turn it into a brief body language lesson. Then get out your toy dog.

Who goes first?

Here are three traditional, well-known methods to determine which couple or team goes first:

- Rock, paper, scissors
- Toss a coin
- Roll dice

Other methods might include:

- Players draw a domino out of a jar, add both of the numbers for a score. High score goes first.
- You can ask a group "Who's got a birthday this month?" If no hands go up, go on to the next month. If there's more than one birthday in a month, go by earliest day. Avoid talking about years!

With any of these methods, decide ahead of time if the winner automatically goes first or if being named winner gives the right to choose whether to go first or not. What is the best use of your time? Playing games or choosing sides? If not done efficiently, choosing up sides can eat into your schedule!

What about team leaders?

If you divide into teams, it helps with the flow of the event if each team has a leader. Not everyone is up to the task, so to avoid embarrassment, ask for volunteers. First announce the job description so they know what they're getting into. Rather than team leaders chosen from among the ranks, you might assign an Assistant Game Leader to each team. Some helpful responsibilities for the team leaders include being sensitive to limiting issues with the humans: Sore back? Hearing deficit? In addition, be sensitive to limiting issues with the dogs: Has he been taught this exercise? Is he sound sensitive? Is he having space issues? AGLs should encourage members to feel free to opt out of a game if they feel it's inappropriate for their dog. They should also be ready to organize a batting order within the team: Which couple goes first, who goes next? AGLs should monitor stress and inform the GL if they see a dog being pushed too far in the name of fun or training.

The use of music

Music is a nice touch for your games session. It's also an effective means of group organization: Start music, relaxation music—but pulling this off can become unwieldy unless you have a designated AGL in charge of the tunes. Classics, rock-and-roll, marches, or sporting events music are all good—anything with a happy beat can encourage enthusiasm for the action parts of your game. For a little added pep, download some stadium sound effects—you know rah-rah, applause, cowbells—play a snippet at the end of a game. A coachable moment: Let the people know a strange noise is about to occur so they are ready to act accordingly with their dogs. You can find sound effects for free on audio clip art. Caution: It becomes difficult to talk over music if you need to give directions—the AGL should be ready to turn off the music when the GL needs to explain something.

Good for take drums confidence building. Noise + desensitized

Sensory overload: Time for a chill-out break

Sometimes the competitive aspect of human nature gets in the way of common sense. The GL should take the supervision of participants seriously and intervene when necessary. Keep some relaxation music on hand for a calming session between exciting games. When people and dogs become too excited, accidents can happen. Intermission for some gentle doggy massage and quiet music can maintain sanity in the group. Turning on the relaxation music can cue the participants to stop the proceedings, get down to the dog's level and start slow, gentle doggy massage. Remind the folks to breathe slowly, think calm thoughts, be quiet and listen to the music until the GL calls for the game to resume. It's wonderful how the entire group settles down. Stopping everything for a chill-out session of one to two minutes emphasizes that we are in this for the good of dogs and their people, not for competition. Resume where you left off, start over, or change the games to less stimulating exercises.

Is this dog okay?

These drawings depict some early warning signs that a dog might be uneasy about his environment and it's time for a break. Discreetly keep an eye on this dog. Perhaps the game is inappropriate for him and an intervention is needed.

Not all of the behaviors shown here necessarily mean the dog is stressed. They have other meanings as well. Look for

SNIFFING

YAWNING

BLINKING

LICKING

TURNING AWAY

13

clusters of such signals as: trembling when not cold, dilated eyes when there's no change in lighting, or panting even if the dog isn't in a warm environment or exercising. In addition to panting, sweaty pads show up on a dry day as damp paw prints on the floor. The dog may stretch his tongue, drool or lick his lips even though there's not food in the offing. You may see a hard, tense body, especially a clenched jaw or tight mouth. The dog might freeze, lower his body, try to hide. He might scratch himself as if he has an itch, or might sniff the ground even though there's nothing interesting there. He may stand with one front paw lifted or shake off as if trying to rid himself of something. The dog may yawn and blink his eyes or turn his head away from the problem. It's time to see if you can change the environment to help this dog become more comfortable.

Winners/Losers/Prizes

The goal for these games is camaraderie and education. Win-lose games can defeat that goal and produce bad feelings. It's counterproductive if "losers" are eliminated from the game while the other couples continue. The players excluded are likely the ones who need the practice the most! I have replaced the term "eliminated" with "promoted." I prefer promoted as it shows the couples they have an opportunity to improve their skills rather than simply test their skills a second time. Under the heading of "A Coachable Moment" in the games descriptions, I've attempted to identify appropriate educational opportunities for that exercise.

If you prefer the competitive atmosphere, most games are easily transformed by adding a point system, judging for specifically defined criteria or by making it a timed event. You can plan a wide enough variety of games so everyone, or everyone's team, shines at something. Another approach is to use your power as Game Leader to decree a handicap or different rules for participants needing help at their level of expertise. I've been known to change the rules in the middle of a game. The couple that was winning is no longer ahead if you suddenly switch the start and finish lines. I've found that if the participants know you are apt to change the rules mid-stream, they are more apt to concentrate on training and enjoying their dogs than thinking about winning.

One idea is to have enough generic prizes for every dog and award them at the end of the event. Another idea: Award categories can be assigned on the spot by the Game Leader so that every couple gets a first place: Best Tail Wagger, Most Contemplative, Fastest, Good Citizenship, Most Creative, Dog Gone Good Award, The Lateral Thinker, Most Precise, Best Dressed, Tallest Player, Thinks It Through, Most Graceful, Best Problem Solver, Most Petite Player, Get 'Er Done Award, Most Polite, The Comedian. Office supply stores have printer-friendly certificate paper.

A trophy shop can create some ribbons or buttons with your logo on them and the word "participant." Everybody receives one. It's good advertising too. A less expensive way to go is online teachers' supply or sports companies where you can buy a quantity of generic blue ribbons—one for each player.

Another award-giving ploy is to subjectively declare a tie between teams. Present each team with a box of candy, stickers, fancy poop bags or other small, fun or practical gifts. It's best to have a supply of identical gifts so everyone gets the same thing. I've had people comment over which roll of poop bags they got—now I get all the same color and design! If you have a couple of nicer door prizes, pull names from a hat periodically to give those away. Ask local businesses for door prize donations. It will be good advertising for them.

You could award "bonus bones." Cut bone shapes out of cardstock. Children in your family? Multitask by keeping them busy and getting some help with your games props at the same time. This is a good small-motor skill exercise for your children. They can decorate the bones with tiny stickers or crayons. When something special happens during a game, a bonus bone is issued. Participants can collect these in their pockets or treat pouches. During break or at the end of the event they will write their names on the bones and place them in a big dog bowl. At the conclusion of the gathering, draw some bones at random for door prizes. I don't give bonus bones for being first or the best at the games, but for special happenings like good effort, outstanding sportsmanship, helping another person, appropriate handling or effective timing of reinforcement. You might consider starting out by issuing a bonus bone to every participant as they walk in the door. Between games you could ask trivia questions like: Which side of the dog has the most fur? What was the name of the child who was Lassie's companion? How many teeth does a normal dog have? (Be sure you know the answers!) You can also award bonus bones by asking people to produce certain items: the first EMPTY plastic bag presented gets a bone. Ask the participants if they can produce a picture of their own dog. Biggest (or fastest found) picture wins a bonus bone.

How about a charity benefit?

Above we were talking about rewards and gratification for ourselves. Plan ahead. Announce that you will be turning the event's game points into dollars and giving that money to a charity. Ask local businesses to help out by matching your donation. Think about increasing the donation by charging everyone an entry fee that will go to the charity. Be sure to let your players know exactly what charity will benefit.

Instructing strategies

A few years ago I wrote a 400-page book for instructors entitled *Coaching People to Train Their Dogs.* Here are some points from that book that might help you be a more efficient, effective and positive instructor.

Instructional format. The outline or skeleton of your teaching style:

1. Tell them: Auditory

2. Show them: Visual

3. Involve them: Tactile

Tell them (Auditory). Captivate your audience by starting with "The Hook"—an explanation of why this game will be worth playing—what the everyday application and benefits will be. Pitch your message, and your coaching, positively. Stay away from words like "don't" and "no" in your explanations. Those messages are not helpful because they lack information on how to do what you're talking about properly. The negativity could be off-putting. You could replace "Don't..." with "Let's try..." When something goes well, tell your student so. A generic "good job" to the whole group is okay if you can frequently intersperse more specific and instructive encouragement: "Good job, Jennifer, you kept Fluffy's attention on you and away from Rocky." Keep explanations short by deciding what you need to say and then cut it down to make it more concise. Use a notebook, smartphone or an old-fashioned clipboard to create a keyword list you can glance at periodically. This helps prevent your explanations from rambling. One of the main causes of rambling is forgetting what you planned to say next. Keywords on a whiteboard or index cards in your pocket also work. Avoid listing the entire agenda in detail on the board. It's distracting for the players if they are focused on deciphering your notes. They might worry that you are skipping something interesting if you (appropriately!) adjust your game plan to reflect the needs of students and time constraints.

Show them (Visual). A picture is worth a thousand words. Sometimes a quick sketch on a whiteboard is helpful. Plan ahead and have diagrams ready on a large flip chart or a giant wall-sized Post-it pad. While explaining, stay away from terms like "go to the left," "turn counter-clockwise" or "face north" in your directions. Some people have difficulty in processing this type of information. Instead, put up temporary visuals on the walls—hang zebra posters on one wall, elephant posters on another, and use them as reference points: "Everyone on the blue line please. Stand on one of the index cards. Face the elephants." An AGL with a big toy dog on a leash is invaluable for visual demonstrations. When your AGL demonstrates, there are some cases, depending on the exercise, where she should stand oriented in the same direction as the participants—with her back to them rather than facing them.

Involve them (Tactile). Some students learn best when they are given the opportunity to try it themselves. A good example is the proper use of a clicker. This is usually best taught by having the student use the clicker herself to get the timing right. Maintaining a loose leash while walking is another. Coach the couple as they are working on the behavior so they can be more successful rather than dwell on what they are doing wrong. If need be, ask them to demonstrate the behavior again to assess what they have learned.

An AGL with a big toy dog on a leash is invaluable for demonstrations. Be aware, however, that the toy might interest or arouse the dogs. The GL should keep her eye on the students and narrate the actions of the assistant. When your AGL demonstrates, there are some cases, depending on the exercise, where she should stand oriented in the same direction as the participants—with her back to them rather than facing them. The AGL's left is now also the students' left, making it easier to follow along with the demonstration. In some instances, this doesn't matter at all.

Involve/coach them. Often students haven't learned exactly what you thought you taught them through your explanations and demonstrations. Comprehension check: If you ask a person to repeat the instructions in her own words or show you the steps she learned, you can spot something that has been misunderstood. You can identify a specific part of the exercise that needs to be changed, isolate it, improve it and insert it (I.I.I.) back into the whole. Explain what the couple needs to do to be more successful rather than dwell on what they are doing wrong.

"Are there any questions?"

It's appropriate to ask for questions, but be aware that questions (and stories!) can eat into game time. "Are there any questions?" can be an opening for irrelevant stories and derail your goals. With practice you can become adept at asking for and answering questions politely and effectively without unnecessary delay. Rather than a generic "Are there any questions?" be more specific and ask, "Are there questions about what to do when it's your turn to start?" If a question turns into a joke or story, smile, give a one-phrase comment like "that's great," "interesting!" "you're kidding!" and then give a piece of relevant information as you move on. It's a balancing act. Be kind: For some folks an hour at your games event will be the social highlight of their month. Be responsible: If the "story" is something like "I did that once and my dog (you fill in the blank)" thank the person for the information and immediately go on with your agenda. Put their name on your mental or physical "Parking Lot Poster" and don't forget to follow up after class, even if it's simply to provide a referral to someone else who might help.

Whenever I do a class or a seminar, I put a large piece of paper on the wall marked "Parking." Clip art has a variety of cute parking lot illustrations. If it's inappropriate, for whatever reason, to answer a question immediately, I'll jot the question, or the name of the person asking, on the poster to make sure we don't forget to follow up later.

Using a marker when coaching humans

Seldom during a games session will you be without the need to coach someone individually. To help students be more aware of exactly what you mean, isolate one part of the exercise and ask them to focus on only that for the moment. Shelve other issues of importance to be brought out and focused on next, or later. Tell them what TO do, rather than what not to do. Keep your focus point to five words or less: "Focus point: Music stops, give sit cue." When you see that aspect of the exercise being done properly, you can mark it with the word "YES." Ignore incorrect attempts for the moment, (unless of course it poses a danger to the dog or those around him), repeat the focus point and ask them to try again. Earning a "YES" and successfully completing that part of the task will be motivating. For a more detailed method of teaching humans with markers, type "TAG, Teaching with Acoustical Guidance" into your search engine.

Use your time efficiently

The GL is more likely to run out of time than run out of games to play. The clock and grid below will help you organize your time. List what you plan to cover in each five minute segment. Schedule the "important" games first and ones that might require more time to play. Have a series of shorter games in mind that can fit nicely into your remaining time. Try not to run overtime. People have planned their day around other responsibilities. Dogs and people get tired and lose focus. People have to go home as promised the babysitter. Some people might not want to drive at after dark. Fifty minutes to an hour is about right. This usually leaves them happy and wanting more—a good note on which to end the activities.

Getting through the material

05 ....

10 ....

15 ....

20 ....

25 ....

30 ....

35 ....

40 ....

45 ....

50 ....

The Games!

How they appear in the book

The first six games are particularly appropriate for use by the Game Leader to assess the skill levels of the dogs and humans involved in the event. The next games listed in the book focus on basic good manners. After that are games involving more distractions or responding at a distance. That group also has  some retrieving and scent work games mixed in. Toward the end are some games easily adapted for special occasions. Finally, to be fair to both ends of the leash, several games for people only are listed.

Selecting games to follow a theme

Appropriate music, decorations, the right refreshments and prizes transform games into a theme party! Holidays, the changing of seasons, current events—all can be the inspiration to design a special celebration. Plan ahead—when the shops put their seasonal merchandise on sale, stock up on supplies for the next year. Buy appropriate fabric and cut bandanas into 22 x 22 inch squares for each dog (and person?) to wear. If you use pinking shears, you won't need to hem them. How about a "Dog Training Around the World" session? A beach party? An all-sports event? Thumb through this book and you will find games that fit the bill. Your search engine will help you find teaching supply businesses, promotional item companies and party shops, which all offer interesting props and prizes.

Novelty &
Confidence.

Handling desensitization
for vet/Groomer
visits

I Spy

Prerequisites and benefits
We play this game on the first meeting of every Pet Dog Manners class to see how people handle their dogs and how the dogs receive handling. Using each dog's name in this personal way also promotes camaraderie among classmates. Appropriate for assessment.

Set-up
The people are seated in chairs with their dogs, on leash. Keep plenty of space between players. Indicate a "neighbor" for each couple.

Description
The two neighboring couples introduce themselves to each other. The people remain seated and take turns calling out various parts on the other dog's body. That dog's partner touches her own dog in the designated place. Example: Betty with Fluffy and Joan with Star:

> Betty: I spy one of Star's feet. Joan touches Star's foot.
>
> Joan: I spy the base of Fluffy's tail. Betty touches Fluffy's tail.
>
> Betty: I spy one of Star's teeth. Joan touches Star's tooth.
>
> Joan: I spy Fluffy's ear. Betty touches one of Fluffy's ears.

The GL and AGL can demo this game with two toy dogs. Try to stay away from specifying left or right, front or back body parts as it is just one more level of complication and doesn't really matter. Model gentle, slow touches.

A coachable moment

If the GL sees someone's dog is uncomfortable at being touched, end the game there and be ready to move on to the next exercise. Later, in a matter of fact manner, the GL can take that person aside and briefly point out that it seemed like Fluffy was worried about having his paw touched. Follow up as appropriate. Prevent players from changing the rules and touching each other's dogs.

Build into Handling lessa.
> Table - Lifting correctly.
> Novelty for handling/touching areas which aren't as a general rule.

Three-Banana Party

Prerequisites and benefits

Dogs get to practice focusing on their partners in a distracting situation. This is a good foundation exercise to later combine other behaviors, such as enthusiastic reinforcement for "Come When Called." Appropriate for assessment.

Set-up

Provide adequate space between dogs as they might become excited. Each couple needs a leash, food and/or toys.

Description

When the GL says "Begin," it's time for each person to get three full seconds of focus from her dog. The dog should stay within a body's length of his partner, on leash, but anything goes, food, petting, toys. Each person needs to keep the attention of her own dog. If she's not charming enough, he may want to go over to a more interesting person. The GL will count: "One banana, two banana, three banana"—then the time is up!

Game variations

Optional rule: On "Begin," the person says the dog's name and then starts the party. This helps make the dog's name a good thing. The dog can be in any position, but obviously engaged with his partner. Beware of arousal levels. You could make this a "no food" exercise and the human partner must rely on her charm alone.

A coachable moment

Because some people are not spontaneous about giving praise, ask each person to tell you what she plans to do for the three-second party. The GL decides if it will be too distracting for others nearby. Recommendation: no balls unless they are on a rope to prevent rolling into another dog's area. Squeaky toys can arouse other dogs. Beware of food possessive dogs. Jumping around and loud boisterous praise can alarm other dogs. Dog disengages from person? An AGL takes them aside and conducts a brief charm school lesson and/or lessens the distractions for the couple. This is not a "stare at me for three seconds" game. It's generalized, heavily reinforced focus.

Good fa putting value in team relationship

+

To show has much the dog has value in their human partner.

Roll of the Dice

Prerequisites and benefits

Dogs should have experience performing behaviors listed on the die (such as sit, down). This game works on cue response. Appropriate for assessment.

Set-up

Make a large die out of a perfectly square cardboard box; 12 to 18 inches is a good size. You might want to cover it in plain white paper. Draw the customary black dots. On the side with six dots write JOKER. On two other sides write SIT. On another two sides write DOWN. On the last side write PRAISE.

Description

The game is played in small groups of two or three couples. The couples form a row facing the GL or AGL, who spins and drops a large die. Together, all couples perform the exercise written on top of the die for as many seconds as there are dots. Example: The first spin might turn up three dots with a label SIT. The handlers will have their dogs sit for three seconds. If the JOKER turns up, the couple can choose their favorite exercise and perform it while the GL counts to six.

Game variations

If this is a very beginning group, you might want to roll the die individually for each couple. That increases waiting time of others, but might decrease the pressure of being the couple that's holding up the next spin. At first you might forget about asking for the duration. The dogs just perform the behavior and are immediately given their reinforcement.

A coachable moment

This is training, not temperament testing. If you feel it's appropriate, you might get into a brief overview of counter-conditioning: Noise of the die predicts delivery of a treat. It's important to get the sequence of the delivery right: First the dog notices the sound of the die, then a treat is given. Not at the same time, not in the opposite order. If participants are using a clicker, watch for the proper timing of the marker also. Careful, the die clattering on a hard surface may worry some dogs. Mention systematic desensitization and let the people know you are starting at a distance and watching to be sure there are no signs of distress (see pages 13 and 14 on body language). Explain that you will come a bit closer next time as long as the dogs are okay. Quit while you're ahead, don't wait for a reaction.

Tic-Tac-Toe – Pause

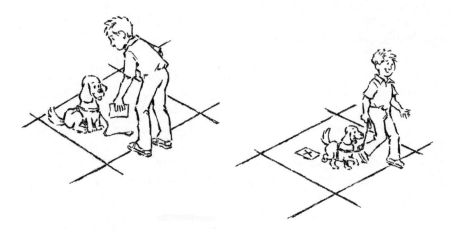

Prerequisites and benefits

Some experience with basic behaviors such as sit, down and leash work is required. The GL can observe those skills. The dog's ability to leave his sideline comfort zone and move to a new location (with all eyes on him!) can also be evaluated. Appropriate for assessment.

Set-up

Create a large (15 x 15 foot minimum) Tic-Tac-Toe grid on the floor. If it's likely that you will use the grid later in a more advanced version of the game, plan ahead when making the grid. The largest dog should be able to lie down with room to spare, not crowding any dog that might be in adjoining squares. Each pair waits their turn at a designated starting place well back from the grid.

Description

Tic-Tac-Toe-Pause is the easiest version of Tic-Tac-Toe. Couples wait their turns at their designated starting point well away from the grid. The GL cues one couple to begin their turn. The person declares a square of her choice and proceeds to walk her dog, on leash, over to it. The dog then pauses, sits or goes into a down, whichever his partner prefers, for a count of three. They return to their starting place.

Game variations

There are several more advanced versions of Tic-Tac-Toe on page 38.

A coachable moment

With assessment games, players should be helped by the staff to be successful at the exercise. Remind them to breathe! If there are issues along the way to the square, the couple is promoted. That means they go back to the starting point to get a private lesson from an AGL while the next pair takes a turn. After coaching, the original couple tries again. The GL can ask the other participants to help out by preventing their own dogs from staring at others. Those waiting on the sidelines can turn slightly away from the team in the middle.

The Stadium Wave

Prerequisites and benefits

Some experience with sits and downs is required so the dog can practice with distractions. Humans practice paying attention to their own dogs plus everything going on around them. "One eye for your dog and one eye for everything else."

Set-up

A line is created on the floor. This is a row in a stadium. Markers are placed along the row. These are the seats. Allow plenty of room between the seats. Dogs are positioned in a sit on the seat markers. Rousing stadium music should be provided.

Description

Choose the couple at one end to start. When the music begins, the GL announces "Score" and the wave begins. First person cues her dog to down and then sit. Number two person in the row is watching them. As soon as the first dog resumes his sit, that signals the next person in the row to cue her dog to go down and up. Each couple begins their down when the dog before them resumes his sit position. Appropriate for assessment.

A coachable moment

Play several times because they get much better as they go along. Praise the group for being able to multitask—watching for their own cue to begin, and then cueing their dog to down, then sit. After observing the participants on the first wave, you might have a short training session. Mention what seemed to be working well and make some comments on how they can improve. Point out the fluency issues of a dog not used to going into a sit from a down position. Give some pointers. This might be a good time to discuss the pros and cons of luring and body prompting.

Trace the Letters

Prerequisites and benefits

A basic understanding of the concept of a loose leash is required. This game helps fine tune the type of leash work needed when dogs need to stay very close to their partners.

Set-up

On the floor, tape the outline of several capital letters. Each letter should be 8 to 10 feet long in print format.

Description

The partners walk together as precisely as possible on the letters. Every time they come to an intersecting line on the letter, they must stop while the dog sits. To trace all of the lines on a letter, the couple might have to double back or retrace a section. The frequent direction changes help both ends of the leash pay attention to each other. Using only one easy letter, this exercise is suitable for assessment.

Game variations

Choose easy letters, like C. It's just one shot and a sit. More challenging letters like A require acute angles and lots of sitting. Someone's birthday? Use their name for this exercise.

A coachable moment

Talk about goal setting and help participants review their criteria for precision heeling versus the more informal leash work. Have an AGL on hand to help couples attain their goal. This might be done by an initial "baseline assessment" run of a letter or two, followed by some coaching, then a second go at the letters.

You Rock!

Prerequisites and benefits

This game gives an opportunity to practice leash work and helps dogs experience proximity to others dogs in a safe manner.

Set-up

Lines, about 10 to 15 feet apart, mark the banks of a river. Designate two teams, each with an AGL as a coach. At two crossing points over the river, install a series of place markers, aka stepping stones, about six to eight feet apart. Each team has their own set of crossing rocks. There should be more than double the number of rocks as there are dogs on each team. This gives each dog several opportunities to sit on a rock before getting to the other side.

Description

The object is for the couples to get from one bank to the other by way of the rocks. The first couple walks (swims!) over to the nearest rock. The dog sits on it with his partner standing next to him. When that dog is settled on his rock, the AGL in charge of that team says "next" and the second couple, giving the dog on the rock lots of space, swims down the middle of the river to the second rock in line and sits on that one. Continue until no dogs are left on the first bank. But there are still lots of unoccupied rocks in the river. The dog on the first rock, directed by the AGL, moves from his rock and swims down the middle of the river to the next empty rock. When he's settled, the second couple goes to the next empty rock and so on until everyone is off the rocks and on the opposite bank. It's almost like leap frog, but no leaping.

Game variations

An advanced version can have the human partner move a short distance away from her dog, leaving him alone on the rock.

If you like competition, the first team to totally cross the river to the opposite bank wins.

For more excitement, if a dog moves from the sit position, the AGL supervising that team can yell "shark, shark" and all of the dogs on that team must return to the starting point. When the alleged shark is gone, it is deemed safe and the dogs begin crossing again.

A coachable moment

The GL can mention consideration of others already on the rocks and ways to make the exercise successful for the entire "community."

Pick a Card

Prerequisites and benefits

Your choice of exercise cards will determine the prerequisites. The game requires calmness and focus during organized chaos. Several couples will perform different behaviors at the same time. It will teach players strategies for politely staying out of each other's way.

Set-up

You'll need a large playing area. Spread the exercise cards face down in the middle of the area. You'll need a timing device.

Description

Set the timer for two minutes. In a group, the couples go into the center and choose a card. They perform that exercise, or, if they prefer, they can put it back face down and pick up a different one. It's important to do the exercise properly! An AGL is watching—and coaching if needed!! The player collects the completed exercise card and goes on to choose another until the time is up.

Game variations

Competitive? The player or team with the most cards when the time is up wins. To make winning more random, write points on the cards and add up the points instead of the number of cards.

Multitask with a larger number of players: Under the supervision of an AGL, half of the couples form the perimeter circle and help their dogs maintain a sit or down while the other half plays the card game in the middle. For every dog that stays, a point can be added to their team's card total. The GL can lead several rounds, but shuffle the deck of cards between rounds.

A coachable moment

As a pregame warm up, have all players perform a couple of exercises together as a group. Training tips can be given at this time.

Green Light

Prerequisites and benefits
Basic skills such as sit and down and walking on leash are helpful.

Set-up
Create a start line and a finish line. Provide plenty of room between them if you have it. Couples cover territory quickly in this game.

Description
Players form a row on the starting line. An AGL is designated "it" and stands on the finish line with her back to the players. The couples line up on the opposite line, facing the person who is "it." The GL starts the game by announcing "Green Light." This tells the group that they can begin walking on leash toward the finish line. At the same time "Green Light" is heard, "it" turns around and calls out a position like sit or down and counts out loud to three. Dogs not in the position at "three" need to go back to the starting line and start over with the next green light. The first couple reaching the finish line wins. You might need to run one section of players at a time. If you play in more than one section, the winners then have a run-off.

Game variations
If you run out of space too quickly, call an "about turn." Players go the other way. The starting line is now the new finish line.

A coachable moment
With this game the GL can illustrate and work on latency (a quick response to one initial cue) and speed (completing the behavior quickly once started).

My Hat's Off to You

Prerequisites and benefits

This game draws attention to excessive body language when a person calls her dog. Keeping her head still helps ensure the dog is responding to the verbal cue, not the body movement.

Set-up

Prepare start and destination markers. Have a flying disc handy for the human to wear on her head.

Description

The dog is left at the starting line. His partner proceeds to the destination marker, turns and faces her dog. She places a flying disc or similar soft, lightweight object on her head and calls her dog without losing her hat.

Game variations

To make it more challenging, require the leash to be snapped onto the dog's harness or collar when he arrives—hat still on head of course! This game could also be modified from a recall exercise into a leash work course.

A coachable moment

As a warm-up exercise, you might want to have the dogs experience the sight and sound of a disc hitting the floor. The GL could turn this into a proper counter-conditioning exercise: The sight of a disc predicts a food treat. Hearing the disc clatter to the floor predicts a food treat.

Flimsy Leash

Prerequisites and benefits

Dogs should have some experience at walking on a loose leash. The game requires heightened focus from the human on the "state of the leash."

Set-up

Organize a safe, confined area with dog-friendly dogs participating. Mark a path of travel. Have plenty of "flimsy leash" material on hand. This can be a length of narrow paper tape or a piece of thread. If you prefer, simply tie a small section of flimsy leash material between the snap and the collar. You'll need some props for the advanced version.

Description

Replace each dog's leash with a flimsy leash. Couples walk around a pre-set course. A broken leash points to the need for attention and focus. The Game Leader will call out directions, mixing them up at will: "walk your dog," "sit your dog," "speed up a little," "dogs lie down," "now go very slowly," or "turn around and go the other way."

Game variations

Advanced course: Be creative and install a few obstacles along the course.

A coachable moment

Explain to the participants about the differences between going for a walk versus more precise, controlled leash work, and the need and application for both cued behaviors. If a leash is broken the partners are not eliminated but "promoted" to a brief lesson with an AGL before rejoining the game. Another option: Give the regular leash back to the couple.

Shape Up!

Prerequisites and benefits
A rudimentary knowledge of basic pet dog manners is helpful. The Shape Up! game allows people to learn by watching others. It helps them get away from dwelling on what's going wrong, and accentuate the positive instead.

Set-up
Prepare stick-on labels by drawing equal numbers of circles, squares and triangles on them. Divide your players into three equal groups by placing a shape sticker on their shirt, making sure you are distributing an equal number of the three shapes. See the information on page 10 for making exercise cards. Divide the cards into three bowls. Each bowl is marked with a square, a circle or a triangle. Mark a circular playing area. Put a place marker at equal intervals on the circle to help players maintain their spacing from other players. This also has them in a position to watch the other players easily.

Description
Arrange the couples on their markers so that their shapes are distributed evenly. For example: circle, square, triangle, circle, square, triangle, etc. instead of all of one shape together. You might do this by putting shapes on the place markers in advance. When all are ready, an AGL pulls a card from the first bowl. Players with that shape label perform that exercise together. Players of the other shapes are instructed to watch any performing couple and make a mental note of something positive about that couple. Those players should be ready to volunteer to compliment that couple when the GL calls for comments.

A coachable moment
The GL might need to role play the first round. Here's a script of how you might get the game started:

> *"Squares, you are up first. Circles and Triangles, please watch the Squares and note something appropriate or effective about one couple's performance. Was the person smiling? Was the person patient when her dog had difficulty? Did the dog respond immediately to the cue? Make a mental note and be ready to tell us about it. Squares, your card says "Cue your dog to sit and walk in a circle around him. Help him remain seated." Ready? Begin. Great! Wow! I have something to say about that! Kristy made sure Brady was steady and focused before she started her trip around him. Good job. Next it's the Triangles' turn to train, so Circles and Squares, be ready. When the Triangles are done, I'm going to ask for a volunteer to tell me something great they noticed."*

Tic Tac Toe – Advanced

Prerequisites and benefits

Some experience with basic behaviors such as sit, down and leash work is required.

Set-up

Create a large (15 x 15 foot minimum) Tic-Tac-Toe grid on the floor. The largest dog should be able to lie down with room to spare, not crowding any dog that might be in adjoining squares. Each pair waits their turn at a designated starting place well back from the grid. Depending on the version, you might need some objects to represent playing pieces.

Description

A very basic version, suitable for assessment, is explained on page 26. It's repeated as the first version of the series of Tic-Tac-Toe games below. All versions give the opportunity to work on good citizenship and community spirit as well as dog training. Teams are selected and designated "O" or "X." In turn, a couple selects one of nine squares in the grid and occupies it. Some type of behavior is then requested of the dog. If played traditionally, dogs lose their turn if they don't complete the task appropriately. I prefer to call this a "promotion," and have them leave the grid for a quick lesson from an AGL. They return to try again later. If playing for competition, the goal is for one team to mark three squares in a row.

Tic-Tac-Toe Pause: This is the easiest version of Tic-Tac-Toe, and is suitable for assessment use. Couples wait their turns at their designated starting point well away from the grid. One by one the GL starts a couple to begin their turn. The person declares a square of her choice and proceeds to walk her dog, on leash, over to it. The dog then pauses, sits or goes into a down, whichever his partner prefers, for a count of three. They return to their starting place.

Tic-Tac-Toe Place Marker Version: Members on one team get yellow toys, members of the other get blue toys. Now as they take a turn, the dog sits, the toy goes down as a marker and the couple walks back to their starting point. Talk about strategies for placing the marker and leaving to give the dog the maximum chance of success.

Tic-Tac-Toe Dogs as Markers, Version 101*: Place blue bandanas on all the dogs in one team, yellow on the other team. The GL announces sit or down. One by one, alternating teams, the partners go to the square of their choice, complete the behavior announced by the GL, and remain there together until the game is over. Decide ahead of time what happens if a dog changes position. Perhaps the couple should just stay there and practice. In a more competitive version, that couple moves off the grid.

Tic-Tac-Toe Dogs as Markers, Version 201*: The dogs stay by themselves in the grid while their partners return to the sidelines. Be alert that a dog is not interfering with another dog. Watch for staring! If a dog moves position, his partner takes him to the sidelines and practices. They can try again if/when their turn comes up.

Tic-Tac-Toe Dogs as Markers Alternating*: One team can do downs, the other sits. A different twist: If a sitting dog goes down, that down counts for the opposing team and vice versa.

Tic-Tac-Toe Emergency Down Version*: A player leaves her dog on one side of the grid, then crosses over to the other side. She then calls him to her, but asks him to go down in a preselected square. At least three-quarters of the dog must be in the square. The dog stays for five seconds, then is called to join his partner. A marker is placed in his spot afterward to facilitate the final scoring.

The lights out version: Each square has a battery operated push light in it. When it's his turn to play, the dog has 10 seconds to turn on the light all by himself. His partner cannot touch the light or her dog in any way. Up the level of difficulty by keeping the handler on the other side of the out-of-bounds markers. If dog is successful, an AGL places a team marker next to the light to keep track of which team owns which lights. Three in a row wins. Legal move: When it's your turn, you can get your dog to turn OUT a light owned by the other team. He-he-he.

*Competitive? Now's the time to keep track of three in a row wins! Play again until everyone has a turn.

A coachable moment

The GL can lead a discussion about handling strategies that will make the task easier for everyone participating. Simple courtesies like turning your dog away, not into another dog, when positioning your own dog on the grid can be mentioned. Reminder: "Losing a turn" really means a "promotion" to a brief private lesson on the sidelines by an AGL, then return to try again.

DIY Family and Friends Board Game

Prerequisites and benefits

Patience, creativity and common sense will give the adults the opportunity to influence the younger generation in all things dog.

Set-up

Here's a good arts and crafts and dog training project for the whole family. Replicate your favorite childhood board game on a piece of poster paper. Create the playing pieces, activity cards, etc. Help children create exercises for appropriate interactions with dogs.

Description

A typical goal for a board game is to get your marker to the finish line first. Along the way there are pitfalls, such as "go back three spaces" or "lose your turn." In a doggy version a space might ask you to "draw a pink card" (or blue card). These are exercises you have created ahead of time on index cards. The exercise cards as described on page 10 can be used, but be creative and meet your own needs. You might have a space that says "Whoops, you didn't close the gate properly, go back three spaces," or "Great! You have a plastic bag in your pocket, move ahead three spaces." Maybe one space on the board holds a stack of promises. The player landing on that square draws one. Examples:

- I will take my dog on an extra walk this week.

- I will get up immediately and give my dog a treat.

- I will check my dog's teeth for tartar within the next three days.

- I will set the alarm 15 minutes early tomorrow and devote that time to my dog.

Game variations

Class instructors: Rather than focusing on family, make a version suitable for use in a dog training class curriculum.

Monkeys in the Middle

Prerequisites and benefits

Minimum skill with the basics of sit, down, leash work and come will allow players to spend game time moving to the next level of these exercises.

Set-up

You'll need a special set of exercise cards for in-place behaviors only. Create start, middle and finish lines.

Description

Two teams play simultaneously by gathering at corners of the playing area, each facing a center line. One couple from each team walks to the center line where an AGL is waiting, draws a card and calls out the in-place behavior to be done. Some examples of in-place behaviors could include: sit, down, bow, touch, sit up, high five, stand, spin. The dog is then left in a sit at the middle line with the AGL while the human partner goes to the far line and calls her dog.

Game variations

This can be done as a competition by scoring and/or timing the event.

A coachable moment

When the game is over, highlight the strengths you saw. You might, without seeming critical, offer a tip or two for improving weak areas.

Use It or Lose It

Prerequisites and benefits
A foundation of sit, down, stay and come will allow game time to be spent building fluency at these good manners.

Set-up
Start and destination markers. A special set of exercise cards with core behaviors on them such as sit, down, come—no variations, just the basic exercises.

Description
Designate two teams. One team draws a card and then comes up with a real-life application of the exercise on the card. She and her dog demonstrate it, then the other participants try the same behavior. The GL intervenes if anyone comes up with a dangerous or otherwise inappropriate application.

Game variations
Value added: Give an AGL a notepad. The players might come up with new ideas for your own bank of exercise cards!

A coachable moment
Some people are nervous about taking a leadership role. The GL should be ready to help them come up with applications.

Olympic Symbol Game

Prerequisites and benefits

The dogs should be well started at sit, down and leash work. They will get to practice common basic exercises within a small area, using minimal time.

Set-up

Recreate the Olympic ring symbol using five hula hoops. Place a starting line at the short end of the symbol, far enough away that a bit of leash work can be observed. On the other end, place a finish line a leash's length from the last hoop for the recall. Depending on the flooring, the hoops might need to be taped down to prevent slipping or tripping. You'll need some stadium music for sure!

Description

One at a time, the couples negotiate the course ring by ring, including the approach (walking on leash) and exit (recall) behaviors. Be creative as to exercises, but this course has worked well for my students:

> **Start:** The pair begins by walking their dogs from starting line to first ring. An AGL accompanies couple for traffic control and coaching purposes.

> **Ring 1:** A dog steps into the ring and receives three seconds of praise. This keeps things upbeat and downplays competitiont

Ring 2: An AGL then directs the couple to the next ring. The dog enters and sits for three seconds.

Ring 3: An AGL directs them to the next ring where the dog does a three-second down. It's okay if the dog is large—overlapping within a ring is a good experience.

Ring 4: Joker. Trainer decides. (Some choices I've seen: Touch, spin, stand, bow…)

Ring 5: The dog sits and stays while his person goes to the finish line and calls him. You might want this to be an on-leash recall

Finish: The dog sits. Congratulate dog and his person!

Game variations

Each ring could have signage with the exercise on it to help an AGL with traffic control. This avoids confusion and allows the trainer to better concentrate on her dog. Alternatively, a diagram could be drawn on a white board. An AGL can count to three at each ring and also do some coaching if need be. You can increase the difficulty by putting a distraction in some of the rings.

A coachable moment

You might make the rule that if a behavior is not done properly, that couple goes back one ring—they need the practice. An AGL should see that the dog is cued properly to move from ring to ring, rather than have to guess where his person is going next.

Spoon Weave Relay

Prerequisites and benefits

Some experience on leash will allow the players to focus on being more aware of and improving their leash handling skills.

Set-up

A line of six cones, poles or chairs are placed six feet apart. The first person is given a large mixing spoon and something lightweight to put in it. Ideas are: a rolled up sock, a crumbled ball of paper, a small stuffed animal, etc. (Traditionally this was done with a raw egg, which I do not recommend!)

Description

The spoon's handle must be held in the same hand as the leash while the couple weaves through the obstacles, turns around and weaves back to the starting line to hand off the spoon to the next in line. If at any time the object falls out of the spoon, the couple must stop and replace the object, then continue the course.

Game variations

To challenge the dogs with even more distractions, set up two courses side by side and have teams race. Beginners can hold the spoon in the hand without the leash.

A coachable moment

Before the game, have a brief session helping the dogs to remain composed while objects fall nearby. You might want to talk about how to teach dogs to release items from their mouths nicely.

Obstacle Course

Prerequisites and benefits
The dogs should be basically unafraid of novel objects and new situations. The course will introduce obstacles below the dog's threshold for alarm, building trust and confidence.

Set-up
Involve the participants ahead of time, asking each person to bring an "obstacle" to the event—help them think of something appropriate and safe: a hula hoop, plank on two bricks, a tunnel made of cardboard boxes—be creative. Spread the obstacles around the training area.

Description
Dogs take turns, under supervision of the GL, negotiating the obstacles. Be sure to check for safety of obstacles and the manner in which the dogs are handled during the game. If a dog doesn't seem to want anything to do with an obstacle, just skip that one. Later you could talk about the situation from the dog's point of view and perhaps work with the dog a little.

Game variations
Change the theme to a Distraction Course. Each person brings something strange from home. A big doll, a bucket of clam shells, a wind-up toy that squirms around, a kitty litter box, a bag of potato chips, a crying doll baby, a rag sprinkled with vanilla extract. The GL supervises the arrangement of the course and keeps track of interpreting the dogs reactions, offering advice where needed.

A coachable moment
What are reasons the dog might be hesitating? Do a task analysis—break the obstacle down into smaller components and train piece by piece. Get out the clickers and conduct a shaping lesson. Is luring a good idea? Want to get technical? What's the difference between luring and rewarding a behavior? Is reinforcement the same as reward?

Good Citizen Puzzle

Prerequisites and benefits

A stable temperament, knowledge of basics and experience on leash will speed progress adding fluency to these behaviors. The dogs practice Canine Good Citizen test items chosen at random. This might spark interest in working toward the CGC certification in the future.

Set-up

For the puzzle, draw the CGC logo on cardboard and cut it into as many puzzle pieces as the program has exercises. A different test item is written on the back of each piece.

Description

This game gives people an introduction to the exercises included in the Canine Good Citizen test. Participants select pieces at random and perform the test item drawn. The puzzle goes together piece by piece and you can congratulate the "collective" good citizen group.

A coachable moment

Depending on the needs of the participants, conduct a brief session on how to get started on training a couple of the exercises. Make the people aware of CGC opportunities in your area.

Wheel of Fortune

Prerequisites and benefits

In this game, the exercise cards you create will dictate the prerequisites required. The main benefit is that it is just another way to make training fun.

Set-up

You'll need exercise cards (see page 10) and a timing device. Provide a full water bottle to act as a spinner. If the ground is not smooth, you might need a large plate to place the bottle on so it spins freely. Space the cards on the perimeter of a circle drawn on the floor. Place the spinner in the middle. The players form a larger outer circle beyond that.

Description

Each couple takes a turn spinning the bottle. When it stops spinning, an AGL reads the card to which it points and the couple performs the behavior.

Game variations

Create competitive teams and have a value on each card.

A coachable moment

Another option is to keep track of speed and latency of the behavior, explain the difference and how to improve both. If playing competitively, a deduction from the value of the exercise can be made. Deduction examples: if the dog takes longer than a second to begin responding to the cue—latency deduction. If the dog takes longer than two seconds to complete the behavior once he begins the behavior—speed deduction.

Hockey Hat Trick

Prerequisites and benefits
Some previous success with polite behavior on leash will help the couples meet the challenges of the ice rink.

Set-up
Create an ice rink by marking two U-shaped hockey goals on the floor at opposite ends of the area. Taping rolled up towels to the floor in a U shape will help guide the puck into the "net." In front of each goal place a large stuffed animal. These are the goalies. If you don't have a really big toy, put the smaller animal on a stool or box. Get three hats of any sort and place them around the rink. The hats could contain balls, food or anything that might make them more attention-getting to our canine friends.

Description
Teams line up behind their goal line. Flip a coin. The first couple is given a broom for a stick and a Frisbee for the puck. That player must push the Frisbee from the starting line, with the dog ignoring the hat distractions, into the net. The dog must remain on a slack leash throughout the entire time or must leave the ice. (They should receive a quick private lesson by an AGL, then return to try again.) The broom and puck are handed to the first player on the opposite team. Play on.

Game variations
Simpler: Reduce the degree of difficulty for the dogs by turning it into a hockey game instead of the Hat Trick Game. Remove the three distraction hats.

More challenging: Increase the difficulty if you are playing with friendly dogs by having both teams start at the same time from opposite ends of the ice rink. If you are competitive, use your imagination for scoring rules.

A coachable moment
Talk about the strategy for solving this problem. One good plan is crossing the ice in little segments by asking the dog to sit and then propel the puck forward a bit. Together, the couple can walk calmly to the puck and repeat until scoring a goal. Some participants might opt for pushing the puck along continuously in little taps. Others might try to get the puck into the net with one gigantic push.

Four on the Floor

Prerequisites and benefits

A stable temperament and trust in one's partner helps. This game helps people to be lateral thinkers and to set no limitations when none are imposed. It's about creativity.

Set-up

Put a piece of masking tape down on the floor, about 30 inches long and 1 ½ to 2 inches wide.

Description

Announce the task very specifically: "Put four feet on the tape." No other explanation. Don't answer questions! Just repeat: "Put four feet on the tape." Each person will have a different idea of what these instructions mean. That's okay. Tell them the only limitations are humane ones. Encourage them to think outside of the box. The GL should intervene if a dog seems ill at ease with the process. There are at least 30 ways (probably more) to safely and successfully fulfill the criteria of "Put four feet on the tape." Show your appreciation for all attempts!

A coachable moment

It defeats the purpose to conduct a training session or give hints before the game. However, when the group seems to be out of ideas, give the dogs a rest and have a brainstorming session to come up with other ways to put four feet on the tape. You can provide toy dogs for this challenge!

Waltzing Matilda

Prerequisites and benefits

Please read this definition first so the game makes sense: "Waltzing Matilda" is an Australian folk ballad about a guy walking through the bush. He's carrying his gear and sleeping bag rolled and tied into a bundle (that bundle is called a swag) thrown over his shoulder. He has named his swag "Matilda." This game helps to teach your dog to accept mild restraint. It provides practice staying put while his person is busy doing something else.

Set-up

Download the music! Divide the group into teams. Mark a starting and ending point for each team. Place a swag in the middle of each path. Swags can be made from a beach towel and a leash, or a piece of cloth and a string. The teams line up single file at their starting point.

Description

The first couples start down their path. When they come to the swag, they unroll it and stretch it out while their dog remains under control. The dog is then asked to lie down on the towel while his person covers him up and counts to three. The dog is then uncovered and again, stays somewhat still and cooperative, while the swag is put back together and left for the next team member. Repeat until all couples from both teams have had a turn.

Game variations
You could have each team carry their own swag over their shoulder to an X marked in the middle of the path, perform the exercise, roll up their swag and proceed to the finish. You will need a helper to carry the swag back to the next couple in that team or provide extra swags to prevent too much waiting around.

A coachable moment:
Point out dogs that tell us by their body language that they could benefit from a rerun. Have the couple go again, but split the task into smaller, point-of-success goals. Coach a high rate of reinforcement.

Thread the Needle

Prerequisites and benefits

The dog should have a high threshold for startle in novel environments and trust in his partner. Thread the Needle helps build trust in unusual situations.

Set-up

Designate start and destination markers. Place a few hula hoops on the floor. Be sure to provide the large sized hoops.

Description

The human picks up the hoop and both partners must pass their bodies through all of the hoops one after another. Difficulty will depend upon the number of hoops you provide and the number of repetitions requested.

A coachable moment

We don't want to ask our dogs to do something that might be frightening. They trust us to keep them safe. Before the game begins, you might spend time getting the dogs (and people!) used to getting through hoops. Ask participants to watch for possible emotional signals from their dogs that they are beginning to be uncomfortable. Help them come up with alternative methods to get the job done without frightening the dogs. Example: The dog can sit while his human partner lowers the hoop over him, and the dog can then walk out of the hoop while it's flat on the floor. From most dogs' points of view, faster is not better for this exercise.

Bandana Relay

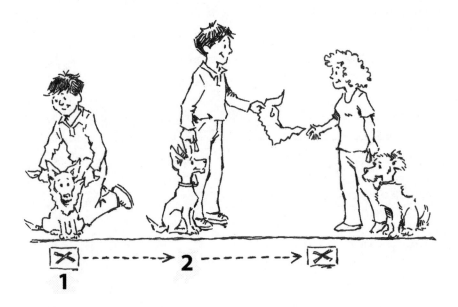

Prerequisites and benefits

Dogs should have a little experience at being willing to stay put for a few seconds. Bandana Relay gives the dogs the opportunity to accept "being messed with."

Set-up

Originally I called this game "Cowboy Relay" and used the typical paisley print cowboy bandanas available in most variety stores. Then I started buying specialty material depicting various themes: seashells for a beach party, hearts for Valentine's Day, fall leaves, etc. You'll need enough for two bandanas and maybe some spares. With pinking shears, cut squares in the typical size of a bandana, 22 x 22 inches. You can diagonally cut the square in half and save material by producing two single-layer triangles. Set the game up for simultaneous play by two teams. Prepare a playing area consisting of two opposing lines long enough to allow for twice as many place markers as there are players. There should be a vacant marker across from each dog—that dog's destination point.

Description

The GL sets the criteria for a "stay." Perhaps it will be a sit. Perhaps the dog will simply be required to stay calm and happy in any position on his marker. The first person in each line holds a bandana. When the game begins, she ties it on her dog, then they walk together to the opposite line where the dog is placed on his designated sit-stay marker. The bandana is taken off the dog. The dog remains on his new marker while his partner takes the bandana back to her waiting teammate. That teammate then ties the bandana onto her dog. Repeat until all the dogs are sitting nicely on the new line, the last one in line wearing the bandana. An AGL should be on hand to supervise the waiting dogs. If a dog is having trouble staying, the play on that team stops while the dog is helped to regain composure. This adds a competitive aspect to the game if it's a timed event.

Game variations

If the participating dogs can't manage the distance from their people try the version which is depicted in the illustration on the previous page. That person ties it on her dog, unties it and passes it on. No one crosses to the opposite line. Depending on the spacing of the markers, there can be a step or two during the pass, or none at all.

When the game is over, it might be nice to give each dog a bandana to take home.

A coachable moment

Some dogs might benefit from a session before the game. Talk about breaking the tasks into smaller steps and reinforcing each of those steps: Allow them to sniff the bandana, touch them with it, then try tying it on. Point out body language that suggests a dog might not be having a good time.

Dress for Success Relay

Prerequisites and benefits

This game is for dogs that won't be bothered by having their heads worked with. The dogs gain experience and are positively reinforced for being handled. This exercise contributes to building the dog's trust of his partner.

Set-up

You'll need start and destination markers for each team. Take a trip to a garage sale or a Goodwill shop to collect a variety of sizes of t-shirts. Spread the shirts around at the destination markers.

Description

The first couple from each team walks together to their team's pile of shirts. The partner dresses her dog in a shirt of an appropriate size, and they walk together back to the starting point. When the first dog is undressed, the next couple leaves the starting line.

Game variations

For beginners you might eliminate any walking to and from the pile of shirts. Instead, just give each couple a shirt and have them dress their dogs.

A coachable moment

The Game Leader could mention the effectiveness of systematic desensitization and/or counter-conditioning. Show participants how to gather up the shirt to form the neck opening into a ring to minimize dragging the shirt over the dog's face.

Blind Man's Bluff

Prerequisites and benefits

This game is for a small group of people and dogs already quite familiar with each other and dogs happy to be handled by others. The main benefit: fun for a few good friends.

Set-up

Each AGL holds a dog by the leash. Their human partners are blindfolded and seated on chairs a slight distance away.

Description

Dog #1 is brought over to the line of seated people and walks past them, pausing for three seconds in front of each individual. The person extends her hand and when the dog makes contact, she has three seconds to feel the dog on the head, then shoulders only. Repeat with Dog #2. How were the folks at guessing which dog was theirs?

Game variations

Make the game more challenging by having the folks wear socks on their hands.

A coachable moment

Will the dogs be okay being touched by a faceless, handless friend? How about a pre-game practice with each dog's own partner using a blindfold and socks?

Monte Carlo

Prerequisites and benefits
The canine players will be asked to practice holding a stay near other dogs.

Set-up
You'll need to make a large die (see page 24). Your die should have Sit, Down, and Joker marked on its sides. Create a playing field by marking six parallel lines about three to five feet apart. The lines should be about 15 feet long. One line should stand out in some way, a different color or width perhaps. This is the "GO BACK TO START" line.

Description
Divide the group into teams, select a running order and assemble them near the start line. An AGL rolls for the first team. The first couple on that team progresses the number of lines as shown on the die and assumes the position displayed on the die. Once the dog is settled into position, his person leaves him there and proceeds to a designated waiting place. Perhaps you'll have them go to a wall or a sideline, or "take ten giant steps" away from the dog. Should the couple land on the "GO BACK TO START" line, they must automatically leave the field, go to the end of the group of waiting players and be ready to try again. When the first couple is all set, an AGL rolls for the next pair. Repeat as above. If a dog happens to break position, his team freezes as that dog's person gets her dog and takes him back to the end of the starting line. They can practice while they wait and then take another turn. Expect the possibility of a traffic jam with two or three dogs on the same line! The hardest part of this game is for the GL to remember whose turn is next, because the players are all over the place. Solution: Have the players take on that responsibility themselves! First team to get all of their dogs off the course once wins.

Game variations
To make it a bit easier, rather than leaving the dogs alone on the lines, the couple can stay together.

A coachable moment
Talk about how good manners will have each couple position themselves on the lines so as not to be directly face to face with each other.

Please Pass the Spaghetti

Prerequisites and benefits

Dogs should be able to be in close proximity to other people and dogs. The game provides the dogs opportunities to practice maintaining composure in a novel situation.

Set-up

There should be two lines on the floor, one for each of two teams. You will need a ball of heavy yarn for each team. Have extra yarn on hand to attach an extension on the end if you run out of yarn before you run out of people.

Description

Dogs must maintain a sit while one by one their partners connect each other with the yarn. The first person might loop the spaghetti around her arm and pass the remainder to the next teammate. That person can perhaps pass it through her belt. Next person in line can thread it through her sleeve—whatever is possible, until all are connected in some way.

Game variations

Be tempted to include the dogs in the process only if you know for sure you have very stable dogs and savvy people.

A coachable moment

Help people remember that even though they need to work with the spaghetti, their first concern is their dogs. Have the people be proactive rather than reactive, helping their dogs to be steady in the face of "weird stuff happening."

Like a Statue

Prerequisites and benefits

A cooperative and trusting relationship between partners is helpful. This game gives the dogs experience at accepting and being reinforced for some gentle positioning.

Set-up

This game requires special "exercise cards." Find pictures of dogs in old magazines or from the internet. Look for dogs in various positions. Easy positions like sit, stand or down are okay, but be sure to get some strange positions such as dogs up on two feet, on their backs, or with their heads just so on their paws. Print or paste each photo on a piece of paper to form a large deck of cards.

Description

In turn, participants draw a card and help their dog assume that position for a duration of two seconds.

Game variations

Competitive? Give each card a score in relation to its difficulty. This is actually a random method of assigning points since what's easy for one dog could be challenging for another. Be sure the spectators get to see the cards.

A coachable moment

If you include a coaching session in this game, talk to the group about how head position can help with positioning the body. "Where the head goes, the body follows." This is also an opportunity to talk about or practice target training—a nose to hand or nose to target stick could help with positioning.

Hound Dog Hula

Prerequisites and benefits

The dogs should be able to experience novel situations without undue stress. They will get to practice impulse control, attention to partner, or perhaps "leave it" if the dogs know this skill.

Set-up

Island music is a must. Reasonably priced skirts and accessories can be purchased online from party stores. Better yet, take a trip to Hawaii to get one. They're sold in every souvenir shop. You can make a grass skirt yourself by cutting strips in a length of heavy brown packaging paper. It will be fragile, though. It's more durable to cut strips in a length of cloth. With strings, hang distractions from the waistband at varying nose levels. Dog biscuits, tennis balls, strips of jerky or string cheese all work well.

Description

An AGL dresses up in the grass skirt. This hula dancer does his/her thing while the couples take turns walking around the dancer with the dog closest to the dancer. One point off for a glance, two points off for sniffing. If there is a grab, the couple is promoted to a private lesson and is able to return for another try. Decide ahead of time if you are going to allow an eye contact/focusing exercise before their trip around the hula dancer or just go for it and see what happens. Will you allow a "leave it" cue during this exercise?

A coachable moment

A pre- or post-game session on attention exercises or how to train and reinforce incompatible behaviors might be appropriate. If a dog looks like he wants to grab a biscuit, talk about being proactive instead of reactive and ask the dog to turn away and sit. Reinforce the sit heavily, then move on around the hula dancer.

Get a Grip

Prerequisites and benefits

The dogs should understand the concept of stay. They will get a chance to practice impulse control for stays while their partners are on the floor fiddling with a bowl of food.

Set-up

Place a line on the floor. About 12 inches beyond the line, place a bowl containing three large ROUND dog kibbles, an empty bowl and a pair of chopsticks.

Description

While the dog waits, with his nose or toes on the line, his partner must transfer the kibble with the chopsticks to the empty bowl.

Game variations

Run two or three couples at a time.

A coachable moment

Not much you can do in a short amount of time regarding people without chopsticks expertise! If it becomes too painful, I'll go over and bail them out by dumping the kibble into the other bowl.

Spot On

Prerequisites and benefits

Dogs should have some experience with sit, down and walking nicely on leash. Good timing of cues and need for low latency in cue response is made apparent by the Spot On game.

Set-up

Define a walking perimeter large enough to keep crowding at a minimum. Spread a couple of decks of playing cards face down in the middle.

Description

Couples walk to the music. When the music stops, all of the couples stop, go to a card and have the dog cover it up with a sit or a down, whichever the GL calls out. This is a precision exercise: If the dog was successful at making the card disappear, the couple keeps it. An AGL will be checking! If not, they simply resume along the walking path when the music starts and they try again for another card the next time.

Game variations

To make it more competitive, add up the total of the value of the cards collected.

A coachable moment

People must take care to keep out of the way of other couples as they choose cards— talk about "one eye on your dog, one eye on everything else." Demonstrate splitting two approaching dogs by turning away so that the person is between the dogs.

Baseball

Prerequisites and benefits

The dogs should have some skill at maintaining duration for stationary behaviors. The game will allow the dogs to practice behaviors among lots of distractions. It also keeps large groups busy simultaneously.

Set-up

Prepare a sack of about 10 old tennis balls. With permanent ink, write OUT on a couple, HOME on a couple, and on the rest write 1, 2 or 3. Mark out a baseball diamond, with home plate, pitcher's mound and first, second and third bases. The bases can be almost any flat object that will not shift position and cause runners (who will not be running) to slip. The bases don't need to be very far apart. Positions Sit, Down and Sit can be written on the three bases. Divide the group into two teams.

Here are some ideas for behaviors to perform on the bases for the batting team and next to those are sample distractions that could be provided by the team in the field:

- Sit on first base. Auditory distraction: Squeaky toy, crinkling of a bag of chips.
- Down on second base. Visual distraction: Wave a flag, move a child's pull toy.
- Sit on third base. Olfactory distraction: Food is offered from a large mixing spoon a short distance from the base. Spray a tiny puff of cologne a distance from the base.

Description

This version of baseball is suitable for a small, indoor space. Half of the participants are up to bat and the other half in the field. Give each the name of a pro team in your area. You might even want to prepare team bandanas for the dogs! The first dog sits on home plate, on leash, at his partner's side. Without looking in the bag, the pitcher takes out a ball and gently throws it to the hitter (the human!) to catch. The dog must stay in a sit while the ball is being caught by his partner. If the person drops the ball, or the dog changes position, that's a STRIKE. Three strikes and that player is out. If they get a "hit" (catch the ball successfully while the dog stays), the owner tosses the ball back to the pitcher. Dog must stay. Once the pitcher has the ball again, the dog/human couple must go to the base indicated on the ball (1, 2, 3, Home). The dog assumes the appropriate position on top of the base within three seconds of a single cue, or is out. He must remain on base in that position until the next batter hits. Then the game goes on. Only the dog at bat performs the exercise. Those already on bases, simply "run" the bases. At each base, a member of the other team is assigned to provide a distraction.

Game variations
No base distractions will make the game easier for both teams.

A coachable moment
Point out to the team in the field that their distractions are going to affect their own dogs. It's a great opportunity for them to train. Remind them to be alert and proactive to this challenge.

Safari

Prerequisites and benefits

An ability to sit and stay at a distance is helpful. The dogs get to practice sitting on a strange surface while their partners are away. This game provides a good photo op.

Set-up

On card stock, print out a quantity of African animals, one each on a sheet of paper. Be sure to make at least three or four copies of each animal. Mark a walking circle or square with a large area in the middle. Half of the animal photos are placed along the path, the other half scattered in the middle. Be sure to have fairly equal numbers of the photos of the same animal on the path and in the middle. Jungle music or African drum music is fun for this game.

Description

When the music plays, the teams walk along the path. When the music stops, they move forward to the next animal. The dog is left sitting on that animal while his partner finds a similar animal in the middle and stands on that. Return to the dogs when the music begins. Repeat. Photo op! People love photos of their dogs. The Safari game lends itself nicely to this. AGLs can position themselves to get a shot of the happy reunion.

Game variations

For atmosphere and added distraction, place a few toy stuffed African animals around the area. For very advanced dogs, the GL could have the dogs called, one by one, back to their partners. When the partners are reunited, an AGL could be on hand to snap a photo of the moment of the happy reunion. Be sure to share the picture with the couple via email.

A coachable moment

Talk about how cameras and photographers can be off-putting to dogs.

Pizza Delivery

Prerequisites and benefits

A basic understanding of maintaining a sit with distractions is helpful. Doors can be a challenge for dogs. This game helps dogs practice appropriate impulse control and good door manners.

Set-up

Save an empty pizza box or two. The greasy kind with melted cheese stuck to the bottom is the best! You'll need a doorway. Player is sitting on a chair on one side of the door, an AGL with the pizza box is on the other. Place a carpet square as a target near the chair. Prepare a change purse or wallet with money enough to pay for the pizza. Optional: Use a cheap battery-operated door bell.

Description

The "pizza person" knocks on the door or rings the bell and hollers, "PIZZA!" The partner gets out of her chair, cues her dog to sit on the carpet square, then lets the pizza person in. The main focus is dog training, not being polite to the delivery man. Help the dog succeed.

Game variations

The delivery man states the amount due and the customer must find the correct amount in the provided purse and pay for the pizza while the dog stays. To add duration to the dog's sit-stay, surprise the participant by having foreign money in the purse, or make sure the correct change is not available.

A coachable moment

A task analysis will reveal lots of components to this exercise. You might work on a few of these in a group as a warm up for the actual game: sitting on a target for a treat, hearing a knock and receiving a treat, sitting still while a door opens and closes. If the participants are using a marker, check to see that their mechanics are correct. Doors are tricky for humans too. Beware—once I found myself locked in a closet while playing pizza delivery man.

Dueling Dogs

Prerequisites and benefits
An ability to maintain a sit and then a down until released is a good foundation for Dueling Dogs. The participants practice sit-stay, being left and then going into a down position.

Set-up
Couples are back to back with a generous distance between them. Option: Some type of see-through partition to place between the dogs.

Description
On a cue from the GL, both dogs stay while their partners walk three steps forward, turn and face their dogs. The GL says "NOW" and both people cue their dogs to drop. Last one down leaves. Another pair comes up and challenges the couple remaining.

Game variations
Instead of a duel, you can play Dueling Dogs as a group by having couples walk around a marked circle. When the GL says "NOW," dogs should drop into a down position. It's more fun to do this to music.

A coachable moment
Promote each dog that is "eliminated" to a brief private lesson with an AGL. After a bit of coaching and practice, that couple can return to challenge again. If you want to get technical, this game gives you an opportunity to talk about and work on:

- Latency (response time between cue and the beginning of the dog's action)

- Speed (the time it takes the dog to complete the behavior once he starts)

- Precision (conformation—does he creep forward or stay put? Do you care?)

It's a Wrap

Prerequisites and benefits

Dogs with experience being handled are asked to remain comfortable with the distraction of having new clothing items put on in the presence of other dogs.

Set-up

A line for each team. A length of holiday material and some ribbon, enough to go around the belly of the largest dog.

Description

Dogs on each team line up on their own line. A dog is wrapped in the material and ribboned, then unwrapped, and the material passed on to the next player on their team.

A coachable moment

Pre-lesson possibility: Introduce the dogs to the ribbon and material by allowing them to see, sniff and feel them. Break the task down into tiny steps and reinforce each step.

London Fog

Prerequisites and benefits
Dogs with a desire to come when called can build self-confidence with the recall behavior.

Set-up
If you opt to play London Fog off leash, provide a safely enclosed area or use a long line. You'll need a couple of large brown paper grocery bags.

Description
An AGL holds the dog's collar or the end of his long line while his person crosses the playing area. Unfortunately, true to form in London, a fog then sets in (the person places a PAPER bag over her head) just before or after she calls her dog. Dog is heavily reinforced for finding his person.

Game variations
I've played with the dog held behind a barrier so he can't see where his person goes. When called, the dog has to find his partner. I like the idea of the dog using his nose as a search aid, but being held while his person disappears can alarm some dogs. Know your players.

A coachable moment
Have a group discussion ahead of time and talk about the suitability of each dog for this exercise, and what variations might be better for their dog. Will it be done on leash? A long line? Some dogs become uneasy when they can't see their person's face. Perhaps a little "bag work" before the game is in order.

Let's Tie One On

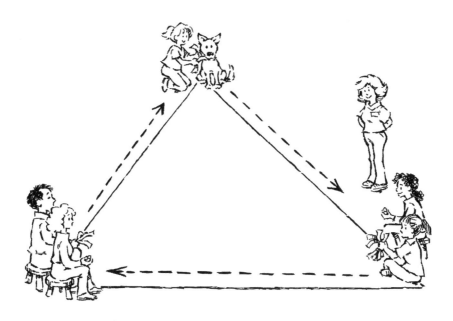

Prerequisites and benefits

This is not a temperament test. Only involve dogs known to be okay with attention and touching from other people. A dog is reminded that people touching his collar is a good thing. This is helpful should someone unknown need to handle the dog some day.

Set-up

Indicate the points of a triangle on the floor, about 10 to 15 feet per side. A long line or an area surrounded by partitions is needed. Prepare a supply of wide, soft ribbon cut into six inch lengths. You will need four staff members for this game. An AGL can participate, but you may need to invite a couple more dog-savvy people. Recruit folks who will follow your directions. It's not a good idea to spontaneously invite unknown spectators for this job.

Description

The staff members form two two-person stations at two points of the triangle. They are seated on the floor, or on low stools or chairs. Sitting helps keep them in a friendly position. One person in each station has a handful of tiny dog treats, the other has a hand full of six inch ribbons. Choose a dog and human pair to go to the remaining point of the triangle. She has treats and ribbons too. The dog is on a long line if deemed appropriate. Play begins. The person ties a ribbon to her own dog's harness or collar and gives her dog a treat. Play goes clockwise, with the two-person station calling the dog over. One person can "tie one on" and the other then gives a treat. The sequence is:

- Call, dog arrives.
- Ribbon holder reaches for the collar.
- Food holder gives one treat as soon as collar contact is made.
- Ribbon is tied on while more treats are given.
- The next two-person team calls the dog and repeats the process.
- The dog's partner, on the third point of the triangle, also calls and ties one on.

Having two people keeps the dog steady. It also allows the person doing the tying to do so smoothly with minimal reaching and fumbling around the dog. The GL will monitor the well-being of the dog during the process, and do some coaching or intervene if needed. The dog is called around and around the three stations on the triangle until 30 seconds are up, or until the game is ended by the GL. Then it's the next couple's turn.

Game variations

A more advanced version might have one station "tie one on" without giving a treat, demonstrating intermittent reinforcement. You might see value in having the first caller ONLY "advertise" their treat before calling. I call it a jumpstart. It's a lure. Talk about the pitfalls of lures if you will be using one as the initial jumpstart.

A coachable moment

Here are some points you might want to include in a pregame training session:

- All couples are given ribbons. Organize the position of the dog and his person so that the person doesn't have to reach out for the dog—her dog is close to begin with. For many dogs, reaching is a trigger to back off. We are trying to counter that with this exercise. People "tie one on" their own dog, then give a treat. Repeat.
- Talk about allowing the dog to sniff the ribbon first, rather than intrusively tying it on.
- Coach people to reach from underneath the dog's head instead of over the top when reaching for the collar.
- People can be reminded about the difference between luring and positive reinforcement. This game is not about luring, it's about contingency training. The food treat is contingent upon the dog's action of running up to the caller. I sometimes allow one "jump start" lure for the first call, then luring is outlawed.
- If folks have a clear plastic bag full of treats, the dogs notice that the mother lodes are still out there. Next it's a matter of the dog figuring out how to train the people to share some of it.

Impersonations

Prerequisites and benefits

Working with social dogs that are not bothered by handling is recommended. Dogs can find that they are safe in a novel environment. People are given the opportunity to be coached in the proper handling of their dogs.

Set-up

Provide a few generous piles of miscellaneous "stuff" to get the creative juices flowing: lengths of fabric, toys, soft cord, construction paper and tape, nothing that will be super obvious as to how it might be used. (No Halloween costumes!)

Description

Each dog will impersonate something or someone and have the rest of the group guess what or who it is. You might want to create a specific category: vegetable, movie character, animal, historical event, favorite food, song. Dogs can dress up, use props, or act out clues. It's the most fun when done spontaneously and people have to scrounge around quickly for props rather than have a lot of time to create costumes in advance. Quit while you're ahead. It's not necessary that the dogs greet or even get close to each other.

Memories from past events: A "rather large" black Lab sitting with a green scarf wrapped around his head was an eggplant. A Dalmatian with a white glove stuffed with Kleenex attached to her belly was a milk cow. A Dachshund was asked to lie down in a nest made of a brown coat. A yellow leash was zigzagged over his back. He was a hot dog in a bun with mustard.

Game variations

Print some certificates out ahead of time. Everyone "wins" a special category. A good job for an AGL is making up and filling in the categories as you go along. Some ideas: Best Dressed, Funniest, Cutest, Most Handsome, Most Shocking, Most Realistic, Most Creative, etc.

A coachable moment

If you choose to teach a brief lesson, demonstrate how counter-conditioning works. See a dog in a costume, then receive a treat—in that order. The strange thing predicts a good thing. Explain how systematic desensitization enhances this process: The strange, new thing is at a distance, under the dog's threshold for concern, then brought closer, watching both dogs' body language to be sure both are okay. Review the body language tips on pages 13 and 14.

Beach Party Lim-Bone

Prerequisites and benefits

A degree of attention between dog and partner is helpful. The dogs practice how to ignore distractions and build impulse control.

Set-up

Two sturdy tables about four to five feet apart with a length of two inch by two inch lumber or broomstick stretched between them and firmly attached to the tables with strong duct tape. From that hang a few SOFT, light-weight, but alluring toys. Some might have Velcro pockets containing food. No heavy toys please. Whether you're a rock 'n' roll or a reggae fan, you will find limbo music you'll like for this game.

Description

Dogs are asked to recall under the limbo (lim-bone—get it?) pole without grabbing a toy. The GL can arrange the degree of difficulty for each dog. The idea is to set it up so the dog will be successful. When a dog makes it through, the couple has a party. A three-banana party (the GL counts "one banana, two banana, three banana") to be sure the party is meaningful in length. (See the description of a three-banana party on page 22.)

A coachable moment

To let the dog know he made the right decision to ignore the lim-bone distractions, the GL has similar items in her pocket. When the dog makes it through to the owner, the GL calls "head up" and tosses a toy to them as part of the fun for the party. Hence the requirement of a LIGHT-weight toy! The dog learns going to his partner is fun and in addition she can get him what he ignored (and maybe wished he could have).

Doggy Café

Prerequisites and benefits
The dogs should have suitable temperament for leash work and manners when close to other dogs. Doggy Café provides a break in the middle of a games session. You will train around real-life distractions involving the dinner table.

Set-up
Tables and chairs for the café. Refreshments. Course markers.

Description
Decide on your criteria for a good sit and acceptable leash manners. Mark a large circular walking path. Several couples are invited to walk along the path. The rest of the group is "on deck" in a nearby staging area. When the music plays, the couples walk along the path. When the music stops, the dogs are cued to sit. The first dog to sit properly, as determined by the GL, leaves the floor and goes to the cafe. (They don't need the practice!) A couple from the staging area is invited to take that place and join the next round of walking. When it gets down to three couples on the walking path, the game ends. Those needing practice got some extra time with an AGL coaching, and everyone enjoys refreshments at the café.

Game variations
The café can be in the middle of the circular path to provide everyday distractions for those walking. Those walking need to ignore those eating and vice versa.

Ask people to bring homemade dog cookies and have a cookie exchange. Be sure to bring the recipes to share with all. List the exact ingredients to prevent allergy issues.

Moji Moji Kun

Prerequisites and benefits
Human players need to be safe and comfortable getting up and down from the floor. Dogs playing need to have a reliable high tolerance of close proximity to other dogs and people. This game promotes group cooperation and consideration for the dogs. It requires a bit of athleticism for the people, and self-control for the dogs.

Set-up
Divide the players into two or more teams of about four or five couples each. Each team will need a separate, somewhat private, area to do their planning. You'll need a line taped on the floor. Start with about a 15-foot line, but be ready to extend it as needed by a team.

Description
I know, it's a strange name! Moji Moji Kun was a game show on Japanese TV. It was played by contestants (people, no dogs!) wearing black full-body leotards! I learned this from a Japanese trainer who adapted the TV show into this exercise for training classes: Dogs and their people will use their collective bodies to spell a word while standing, sitting or lying on the line on the floor. Teams can have fun guessing each other's words.

Game variation
Turn it into a special event game by giving teams a theme to represent with their word. For example, if it's spring, the GL might require the word to be some type of spring flower. This increases the difficulty of the exercise somewhat.

A coachable moment

Teams should have an organizational meeting and decide upon a word that works for the skill level and temperament of the dogs (and people!). Interesting aspects of how dogs react to the world around them can be discussed. For example, a dog might be happy to sit next to another, but ill at ease in the down position. Talk about how a dog's body language can show their state of mind. See pages 13 and 14 for information about canine body language. If personal space issues are a concern for a dog, players can be creative and include that dog by assigning him to be a letter that involves only him and his partner, rather than close proximity to others. Some ideas are L, P, T or V, or even an exclamation point. A sitting dog could a period at the end of the word.

Mine or Yours?

Prerequisites and benefits

Dogs participating should have a degree of self-control in close proximity to other dogs. The game provides opportunities for dogs to approach each other and turn away. People practice the real-life skill of making a second choice in deference to others.

Set-up

There's usually a variety of colors in most game-playing environments: green grass, brown tree trunks, trash containers, jackets thrown over a chair, curtains on the wall, bulletin boards. If the existing environment isn't very colorful, cut some bone shapes out of colored construction paper and pin them to walls or trees and scatter a few on the ground. Another way to add to the existing color options is to tie bandanas or ribbons in strategic places in the playing area. This increases the chances for finding the appropriate color quickly and having lots of options and second choices, in selecting a color. Avoid using red. Some people have difficulty seeing the color red.

Description

Participants walk together to music along a defined circular path. The music goes off, the GL announces a color, and each couple finds that color somewhere in the room. The human partner puts her hand or foot on the color and keeps it there as she asks her dog to sit. Sounds simple, but the entire group will be going for colors at the same time. The important rule is that there can be only one couple per object. This is where the "Mine or Yours" comes in. If two couples approach the same object, one must defer, early on. They turn away and find that color somewhere else. It's not polite in people or dog language to rush head on, face to face and try to claim the color first. Establish the rules that color on any human or canine body cannot be used. This includes your own shirt or your dog's leash!

Game variations

Collect the Ribbons: Instead of random environmental colored objects, have a large supply of 6-inch ribbons in an assortment of colors scattered in various places and tied on objects. When the GL calls a color, whoever ends up with that ribbon removes it and ties it on her dog's collar or harness. This version makes choices increasingly scarce, and increases the effort required to remain a good citizen and yield. I would not count up the ribbons at the end to determine who has the most. This puts people in conflict between being competitive and being a good citizen.

I Hear a Symphony

Prerequisites and benefits

The dogs should not be overly sound sensitive and should be willing to interact with strange objects. The game provides the partners a chance to practice task analysis, creative thinking and development of an effective shaping plan. I Hear a Symphony helps students break away from perceived limitations.

Set-up

Collect used toy musical instruments. You'll want more toys than you have participants so each couple can be sure to have several from which to choose. Goodwill has a fine selection—pianos, drums, electronic keyboards, bells, guitars, tambourines—shop around and use your imagination. Spread the toys out in the middle of the area and allow people, alphabetically in order of the dog's names, to choose an instrument. Search the internet for a Motown group called The Supremes—you'll find just the right music for this game.

Description

This game is not appropriate for a one-hour session. It works well in a one- or two-day event because it takes several brief training "rehearsals." Each dog is shaped by his person to "play" his instrument. Five to ten minutes of training can be interspersed with other games and activities during a day-long event. In the case of weekly classes, a few minutes a week can result in a symphony at the end of the session.

A coachable moment

Lead a group discussion on possible shaping plans for teaching each dog to play his instrument. Use a paw to strum a guitar? Use a nose to play a piano? Grab the tambourine and shake it? Can you capture a spontaneously offered behavior and then reinforce it? Can an existing behavior, for example "target," be used to create a new behavior?

Surfin' USA

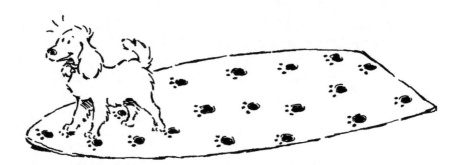

Prerequisites and benefits

The dogs work at maintaining a stand, while in a slightly unusual position, on a novel surface.

Set-up

This is the perfect use for that old foam boogie board you have in the garage! Don't have one? It's okay, just cut a surfboard shape out of a piece of cardboard. If your ironing board is stable when folded flat, use that. Draw 8 to 12 doggy footprints in random locations on the board. Be sure they are spaced at variable distances apart so four of them can be selected as comfortable targets for any size dog. Search the internet for songs from the 1960s by The Beach Boys—you'll find just the right music for this game.

Description

The dogs take turns doing a stand-stay in the paw prints for a few seconds. Due to the location of the paw prints, chances are one of the dog's paws will have to be slightly extended.

Game variations

To increase the challenge, you could require the dog to wear sunglasses and a visor as he surfs. You might draw the surfboard on one step of a flight of stairs. The dog can surf one of the incoming waves.

A coachable moment

If need be, adjust the exercise to a point of success for some participants. Those dogs could sit on the board instead, with only two front feet in easily positioned paw prints.

(Don't) Watch Your Step

Prerequisites and benefits

The dog should have experience walking on leash. This game reveals if more work is needed on the dog's attention to his partner and the fluency of walking on leash. Mostly it's an exercise for people to learn to communicate effectively with each other: As George Bernard Shaw noted, "The single biggest problem with communication is the illusion that it has taken place."

Set-up

Mark the boundaries of a playing area—12 x 24 feet will work. This activity takes a lot of space and is best done one couple at a time, so it is fairly time consuming. You'll need various objects to put on the floor. Use anything that's handy, for example cones, ropes, books, chairs, leashes, coats, purses, toys, boxes and bowls. Use a bandana or other suitable item as a blindfold.

Description

The objects are scattered around on the floor. The articles must not be breakable or dangerous to the dogs or people. Select two couples to work together. One couple has to walk through the course without stepping on or bumping into anything. This is hard, because the person is blindfolded and the dog must follow along closely! She will be given directions by the other player on how to get through the course successfully.

Game variations

This exercise also works well with humans only. I often do it at instructor workshops!

A coachable moment

When folks know who they will be working with, a meeting can take place to plan how to give directions positively and effectively. Input from both is desired as they will take turns guiding each other. How big is a big step? Is it the same as a high step? How should turns be directed? Consider how all of this affects the canine partner! An AGL might want to video the exercise so the blindfolded person can enjoy it later. If you're devious, you can turn it into a "mind" field for the most good-natured player. After the blindfold is in place, an AGL will silently sneak into the course and remove EVERYTHING. When the player is done high stepping and dodging across the empty course, announce "good job," remove the blindfold…and duck. Now THAT will make a good video.

It's the Pits

Prerequisites and benefits

Play It's the Pits with dogs that are somewhat experienced with come when called. Some dogs enjoy playing keep-away, a habit that can be frustrating and dangerous. Reaching out to grab them sometimes makes matters worse. This game makes us aware of actions that promote or trigger playing keep-away.

Set-up

You will need a start and a finish line as well as two quarters (25 cent coins).

Description

In this exercise the dog is left on a stay while his partner walks 15 to 20 feet away. She puts a quarter under each arm. She calls her dog. She must reattach the leash without dropping the quarters clamped in her armpits. The means she can't reach and she needs to motivate the dog to come close.

Game variations

It's the Pits can be played as an individual challenge, a timed event, or in competitive teams.

A coachable moment

If you see couples having difficulty with this, change the game to a version of "Let's Tie One On" (see page 75). Tie One On started as a more simplistic exercise called "Gotcha" that I do in every pet dog manners class. With their dogs on leash right in front of them, the people perform these actions in this sequence:

1. Grab their dog's collar.

2. Use a verbal marker if desired.

3. Place a treat in the dog's mouth.

4. Let go of the collar.

5. Repeat.

It's important that the trainer lets go of the collar before repeating the sequence. This emphasizes the action of the collar grab being the promise that good things will be delivered immediately. In my instructional format, the "Gotcha" exercise is an important component to teaching come when called.

Gold Rush

Prerequisites and benefits

If considering this game, realize that a dog might experience boxes falling down around him. The dogs in your group need to be okay with this possibility. Gold Rush helps the dog learn to be polite for the next time you are walking over an icy sidewalk with arms full of grocery sacks.

Set-up

Repurpose boxes, milk cartons or blocks of Styrofoam packing and turn them into gold bricks and nuggets. If you want to be authentic, spray paint them yellow or wrap them in gold paper. Write a value on each box. Mark a starting line behind which the boxes are placed in a pile—the gold mine. Designate a distinct location across the playing area as the bank. Place obstacles between the bank and the gold mine. Some examples are coat racks to walk under, piles of anything to step over and chairs to walk circles around.

Write a value between five and 25 on each box. Make it easy on the scorekeeper by using increments of five. Think about making the awkward-to-carry boxes higher in value.

Description

Select two teams for this competitive game. The first couple from the first team walks from the bank to the gold mine and picks up as many boxes (gold nuggets) as she dares. She might be greedy and take a lot of gold, but if so she runs the risk of dropping some from her armload on the way to the bank. She must carry the booty through the course, encouraging the dog to walk along nicely. Whichever team deposits the most gold in the bank wins.

Game variations

If a person drops boxes along the way, not only does she lose that gold brick, its value is deducted from her total. A double penalty! By the way, if a player drops a box, a robber from the other team can steal that box and the value is added to her team's final score.

Pair the Socks

Prerequisites and benefits
This game builds fluency in retrieving. While some experience helps, it is not necessary.

Set-up
Here's a good use for odd socks! Every family with dogs has a pile of those. Create a starting line and scatter socks at the far end of the playing area.

Description
Set a timer for a minute or two, depending on how many dogs need a turn. The dogs take turns, one at a time, to go out, grab a sock, return with it to their partner, then the next dog goes. When the time is up tally the score: one point for each sock, five extra points for a matched pair.

Game variations
Include non-retrievers by having their humans go out with them, tuck a sock under the dog's collar or harness and allow him to bring it back that way. Some dogs are enthusiastic retrievers and want to grab more than one sock on their turn. You probably know a dog like this! Decide ahead of time if that dog will be given credit for the extra socks…or penalized for being greedy.

Folk Dancing

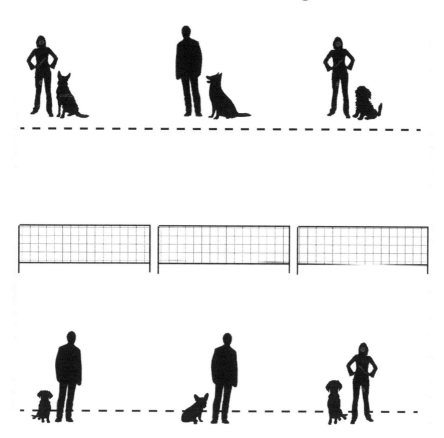

Prerequisites and benefits

Dogs need a degree of attention toward their partners to ignore distractions that will occur during the game. Folk Dancing provides the opportunity to practice being calm while others are moving about in very close proximity

Set-up

Create two parallel lines about 20 feet apart and mark a double center line so there is a "spacer" of about six feet in the middle, since the dogs will be approaching each other face to face. Better yet, the center line should be a see-through barrier—a line of chairs will do if you don't have proper dog class barriers. It helps to have place markers on the lines so that each couple has another couple directly across from them. Turn on some fiddle music and the GL calls out steps.

Description

There are lots of dance types that can be adapted for groups of people and their dogs. It's a good activity to keep large numbers of players involved at the same time. The Virginia Reel is a type of country dance well-suited for dogs. A list of the most simple dance steps follows. Make up your own!

- Tap Toe Right (Left): Dog sits (lies down) by his partner's side while she taps her right (left) toe to the beat.

- Three Steps Forward, U-Turn Home: Walk toward the middle, turn into the dog, return to home line and face middle.

- Airplane Left (Right): Dog sits while partner holds out both arms as wings and circles dog with left (right) hand over dog's head. (Yes, it's possible on leash.) Alternative move: dogs in a down position.

- Forward and Back: Three steps forward, quickly back up to home line, calling dog to sit in front.

- Dog at Sides: Dog returns from a sit in front position to his partner's side.

More challenging steps for appropriate dogs—remove the barrier:

- Pass on Through: Teams walk through each other at the center line and assume a new home line position on the opposite side.

- Swing Your Partner: Walk attentively to middle, hook right arms with the opposite person and swing each other 180 degrees, break off and each couple returns to sit on their home line.

A coachable moment

Explain and demonstrate a step. Practice it without music so you can be heard clearly, and then repeat it with music. When that step looks good, teach another. Note: If the steps require dogs to approach nose to nose, it's wise to provide plenty of room and some type of barrier in the middle. When people get to dancing, they might forget to watch out for each other.

This game allows you to explain back chaining: Teach one step until it's smooth and seems easy and fun for the dancers. Add a new step to be danced BEFORE that original, familiar step. Concentrating on the new step is reinforced by the fun of doing the old, easy step.

This is an opportunity to explain that dogs might find themselves closer to each other than their partners thought. Will these dogs be okay with that situation? If not, what safeguard measures can be implemented?

Pass the Buck

Prerequisites and benefits

This game is appropriate for dogs that enjoy playing with toys. It helps stimulate lateral thinking for the humans.

Set-up

Find a stuffed toy the proper size for all dogs to manage or have a large dog and a small dog team with correspondingly sized toys.

Description

Dogs take turns transporting the toy from the start line to the finish line. They can carry it, drag it, wear it or pull it on a string. Anything goes except having their partner carry it for them. The partner's job is to toss the toy back to the next couple in their team waiting at the start line.

Game variations

A more hectic version would be to design an oval course and have the dogs meet back at the starting point where they hand the toy (the "buck") over to the next dog on the team.

Doggy 911

Prerequisites and benefits

Dogs should have confidence enough to remain calm while walking around in the midst of the action. Doggy 911 helps build a trusting relationship between partners.

Set-up

Designate a starting point and destination point for each team. Make two posters depicting doghouses with flames coming out of the roof, and place them on the destination points. The flames could be red tissue paper. Place a plastic jar by each poster. You'll need several plastic cups, all the same size. Have some extra fun by providing toy fireman's hats and siren sound effects.

Description

This is an outdoor game for a hot day. Divide the participants into two teams. The object is to put out the fire by dumping the water into the jar by the burning house. The fire is "out" when the jar is full of water or when the time is up (GL's choice). Each couple is given a plastic cup to carry water. She tells the AGL how much water to put into her cup. Most people want the cup to be full. That's not always the best idea. She must hold the cup of water in the same hand as the leash is held, and walk with her dog to her team's house and deposit the water into the jar. When that couple comes back to the starting line, the next couple on the team takes a turn. Keep on going until one team fills their jar and the fire is out.

Game variations

A better, time-saving idea: The fire is out and the game is over when a specified amount of time has elapsed (possibly allowing people more than one turn). Another shorter version: The fire is out when each team member has taken a turn. In both of those variations, the water in the jars has to be compared to see which team won. The game can be made more challenging by requiring the fireman to weave in and out of obstacles on the way to the fire.

A coachable moment

It's a good opportunity to discuss the benefits of planning before doing. A full cup of water, for example, is not always the best or fastest way to solve this problem. What about the dog? Will he like water spilled on his head? Will the siren music bother him?

Red Rover, Red Rover,
Call the Dog Over

Prerequisites and benefits
The dog should have experience with the stay and come-when-called behaviors. The game promotes attention and motivation for the dog to rejoin his partner.

Set-up
Create a start line and a finish line appropriate for the level of the players.

Description
All the partners line up along the start line. The person from the first couple leaves her dog in a stay, taking her leash with her. Long lines might be appropriate. The person then calls her dog who, after arriving, sits with his person while she snaps the leash on. Then it's the next couple's turn to play. An AGL is on hand to supervise the dogs remaining by themselves.

Game variations
This game is appropriate for simultaneous team play only if there is room for adequate spacing and the personalities of the dogs are appropriate. Competitive? Play in teams as a timed event. The opposing team can provide distractions. Reasonable

rules for distractions should be set ahead of time—for example distracters can't leave the sidelines, can't touch the dogs, can't throw food or toys. The GL makes sure each dog is successful at reaching his partner and is reinforced appropriately for doing so.

A more advanced version has all of the dogs lined up together on the start line while the people are lined up on the finish line. People call their dogs, one at a time.

A coachable moment

You might want to do some pregame attention exercises. Note: The dogs remaining need to stay while they see another dog running to his partner. The dogs are not all called at the same time!

Musical Chairs

Prerequisites and benefits

The game allows dogs to practice a combination of walking on leash and stationary exercises at a distance. Musical Chairs is appropriate for dogs with a reasonable level of confidence when left alone.

Set-up

An oval or round walking path is marked on the floor. Chairs are clustered in the middle of this area, facing outward. Try to make all chairs an equal distance from the walking path. An AGL needs to be ready to arrange chairs and play music.

Description

I like to start the first couple of rounds with a chair available for each player. Once everyone is comfortable with the exercise, I start removing a chair after each round so there is one less chair than there are couples.

When an AGL starts the music, the participants walk their dogs around the perimeter. When the music stops at random intervals, the GL calls out a position and the dogs are left on the perimeter in a stay, while their people go sit in a chair. Running is not permitted! Dogs creeping into the illegal area or dogs that otherwise break position require their partner to get up and go over to the dog to help him re-position. During that time, the person who was "out" (did not get to a chair in time) can put her dog in a stay and take over that chair. When the music comes back on, people join their dogs and continue walking. During that time an AGL removes a chair. The next time the music goes off, one unlucky person is left without a seat. While traditionally this couple would be "out," I like to keep them in the game by allowing that couple to continue walking with the group, but no longer go for a chair. They do their stays together along the perimeter. They need the practice at a level of success! Commonly, the game is continued until two couples are vying for the one remaining chair. Yikes!

Not a good idea! For years we have been ending Musical Chairs with two remaining chairs, resulting in two winners and less chaos. We instituted this rule after the time we experienced broken legs! Two people, racing recklessly, collided on the one remaining chair at the same time, breaking three chair legs.

Game variations

If you don't have chairs, use footprints cut out of cardboard for the human partner to put one foot on. Caution: Paper can be dangerous on slick floors. Hula hoops also work well, especially outdoors.

Musical dog hoops: Place hula hoops in the middle rather than chairs. When the music stops, the dogs do their stays in a hoop while their partners return to the perimeter. Advanced hoops: When people return to the perimeter, they are directed to walk around without their dogs. Dogs patiently wait in the hoops until the music starts again and their partners return to them.

A coachable moment

A person or two might tend to want to keep pushing their lower achieving dogs to keep up with the others. Monitor the dogs' well-being. Be quick to intervene and change their rules of play to a version (mentioned above) at which they can be successful.

Bullseye

Prerequisites and benefits

The Bullseye game works best with dogs that have an understanding of down at a distance. It's a fun way to practice "emergency downs," sometimes known as Drop on Recall.

Set-up

You'll need a start and finish line. In the middle of the two, create a circle (the bullseye) several feet across. This could be an area rug, a circle of tape, or even a hula hoop. Whatever you use, make sure it's slip proof.

Description

The dog waits at the start line for his partner to cross to the finish line. He is then called across the bullseye and cued to drop so that (hopefully) he hits the bullseye. Score five points if every bit of the dog's body is on the spot, four points if some part of the dog's body is on the spot, three points for the dog dropping within a body length of the spot, two points for dropping at all, and one important point for at least coming when called.

A coachable moment

The ability to drop quickly in any situation is a useful, if not potentially lifesaving, skill for dogs. Talk about the possibility of poisoned down cues. Example: A person might praise her dog for going down on the "Down" cue. The same person might cue the dog to "Down" and then scold the dog and take trash from his mouth. Is the "Down" cue associated with a good result or a bad result? If both, we have a possible muddy situation and conflicted dog. Another concept to share: Ask people to answer silently in their own minds if they are guilty of saying "Down" when they want their dog to get off the couch or stop jumping up on them. It might provide an "Ah-ha" moment in regard to ambiguous cues. "It's best to communicate in black and white, rather than shades of gray."

Baguette Retrieve

Prerequisites and benefits

People with retrieving dogs have the opportunity to test the reliability of their fetch cues in the face of the alternative, which is to eat the bread!

Set-up

Most shops mark down stale bread. Get some stale baguettes and perhaps some bread sticks for smaller dogs. You'll need a bread basket for each team. The game is done as a simultaneous event with two or three teams going at once. One baguette is placed on a marker for each team. The start line is about 15 feet from the baguette.

Description

The first dog in each couple is sent to retrieve his baguette. If he makes it back with the bread, or part of it, it's put into his team's bread basket in a safe place. Each dog gets his own new baguette for his turn. When all are done, line up the baguettes for each team. Longest line of bread wins. Someone takes the bread home to feed the birds.

Par for the Course

Prerequisites and benefits

Dogs with some experience coming when called can practice greater fluency by playing Par for the Course.

Set-up

Mark a start and a finish line as far apart as you want to practice the come. Between the two create the usual features you might associate with a golf course. Several "water hazards" could be made with dog bowls full of water. The dog might be caught up in a "sand trap"—bring in a kitty litter box. Pull up some handfuls of grass and sprinkle it around on the floor for "the green." Potted plants, toy groundhogs and a cookie sheet full of tennis balls can create "the rough."

Description

Rather be golfing than training your dog? No problem! Let's work on come when called and go golfing too. First up leaves her dog behind the starting line, proceeds across the golf course to the finish line and calls her dog. If the dog comes directly on one call without being trapped by a distraction, it's a hole in one.

Game variations

Competitive? Lowest score wins, so a hole in one is one point. Each putt adds an additional point. Cues should be minimized, so a person's extra call, signal, head nod or anything considered additional help each adds one more point. The dog's deviation to a distraction is another added point. If the dogs playing are of different skill levels, use the handicap system or different rules for different players.

A coachable moment

For a pre- or post-training session, help players do a task analysis and break up the exercise. Plan two or three mini recalls by only going part way across the course, avoiding the tricky areas, or plan the tricky area as a destination for the first leg of the recall, giving the partner a little more control over the distraction. The trainer can leave her dog again and proceed to another advantageous location, eventually putt-putting their way to the finish line. You might comment on the benefit of minimized cues. One example is that the dog might consider extraneous body language the salient aspect of the cue. The body movement might overshadow (cause him to devalue) the verbal cue.

Dogzilla Strikes Again!

Prerequisites and benefits

Dogzilla Strikes Again gives players a chance to see how their prior distance control work with their dogs is doing and provides opportunities to think outside of the box. This is one of my favorite lateral thinking games. Developed for my students in Japan, I have played it all over the world and people love it. I hope you enjoy it—the dogs always do!

Set-up

This game requires a bit of advance planning and work. To create a simulation of the skyscrapers in Tokyo, collect about ten narrow, tall cardboard boxes of varying heights, about 10 to 20 inches high. Whiskey bottle boxes and cereal boxes are a good size. Wrap them in plain paper if you have time. With a non-toxic marker, draw windows and doors on the boxes to make them look like office buildings. Alternately, print out some photos of office building walls from the internet and paste them on the sides of the boxes. I like to embellish the buildings with large signs of Japanese businesses: Honda, Asahi, Mitsubishi, Nintendo, Suzuki, Takashimaya. You can even get the logos from these companies on the internet. I usually draw Tokyo Tower on one large box. We all know that was a favorite of Godzilla's. You might consider this artwork a waste of time since, due to the nature of the game, your buildings might have a short lifespan. By the way, make a few extra buildings. Recently, I've made more suitcase-friendly buildings by drawing on extra-heavy hardware store paper bags. They will stay erect if you insert one bag into another so both ends are solid. This double bag makes a sturdy building you can break down and store more easily for next time.

Mark the city limits of Tokyo with tape—a square about 20 feet by 20 feet. Erect the buildings within the city limits. You'll need a timing device and the soundtrack from one of the Godzilla movies. Be careful—I freaked out a couple of dogs once because my first soundtrack had screaming people in it.

Description

The object is for people to take turns getting their dogs to impersonate Godzilla and flatten Tokyo—just like in the movies. The buildings are to be knocked over or taken out of the city limits. Humans cannot step inside of the Tokyo city limits (the boundary lines). Each couple has 30 seconds to try to knock over or out as many buildings as possible. The rules change after each couple's turn. For example, if the first dog knocked over a box because his partner tossed food on top of it, the rules for all of the subsequent players are now 1) humans stay outside of the city limits, and 2) no food can be used. Maybe the next couple takes out a few boxes by retrieving. Add NO RETRIEVING to the list of "do nots" for all subsequent players. The GL supervises carefully to keep all attempts reasonable and safe. Yes, it becomes more difficult to be creative while tackling the problem within the existing rules. An AGL can be the reconstruction crew between turns, setting up overturned buildings and possibly replacing those beyond serviceability.

Game variations

Set up some battery-operated push lights within the city limits. Along with destroying Tokyo, give the dog a point for each light he turns out too.

A coachable moment

At the end of the game, discuss various ideas for teaching a dog to turn out a push light.

The Shell Game

Prerequisites and benefits

This game allows any dog with a nose to use his scenting skills! It's a good opportunity for humans to observe canine behavior.

Set-up

You will need three plastic bowls (the "shells") and some food treats. Arrange the shells, bottoms up, on the floor. The idea is to hide a treat under one shell, shuffle the shells around into different positions, and allow the dog to find the shell hiding a food treat. Point out how dogs rely heavily on their olfactory system to explore and evaluate their surroundings. You might talk about how sliding the bowls around also slides the food all over the surface of the floor, spreading the scent and contaminating the area with residual food scent. Dogs are smart; they can learn to go for the source of the odor. If it makes you feel better, you might tape the food inside the bowl where it won't make direct contact with the floor. A smear of something sticky, like peanut butter, is easier yet. When found, you can turn the bowl over for the dog and allow him to lick off the peanut butter.

Description

While the dog watches, the game leader places the goodie under one bowl and then shuffles the bowls around. Then the dog checks the three overturned bowls on the floor to find the one with the treat. We're not asking for any specific indication. I think the dog will make it clear to you in his own way.

Game variations

It's probably best to set a time limit to reduce frustration. If the dog doesn't find it in 10 seconds, show it to him and let him have it!

A coachable moment

You might make the participant aware of classes in the area that specialize in scenting activities.

Scrabble

Prerequisites and benefits
Dogs with some experience retrieving benefit from the opportunity to build retrieving fluency.

Set-up
Divide into teams. Scatter a set of children's alphabet blocks about 10 feet from each team. Get blocks that are big enough so the dogs can't choke. You can find giant-sized plastic alphabet blocks in a toy store. Have a cell phone handy to check spelling!

Description
Scrabble is a good English lesson for the people and retrieving practice for the dogs. Each dog on the team is sent in turn for a block. The team that gathers letters to create the biggest word wins.

Game variations
Mark the letters with values, just like the traditional Scrabble game! Select a few difficult letters, like Q, Z, V and X, and give extra points for using those letters.

A coachable moment
Have a quick group session to warm up with a few short retrieves. Praise the dogs that released the blocks politely.

Spin the Bottle

Prerequisites and benefits

A "Do It Yourself Craft" game that emphasizes targeting behavior and cue discrimination. The toy can be created in class and the exercise started. Teams can then take it home with instructions to perfect the game.

Set-up

You will need to get some clear, dry, empty beverage bottles with wide enough mouths to allow food to pass through the opening. You'll also need a supply of wooden chopsticks or dowels, although straight, sturdy sticks from your yard could work. You will also need scissors and dry kibble.

Description

Help folks make a toy for their dog with repurposed items. Discard the bottle top, the label and the plastic ring around the mouth. Punch corresponding holes on either side of the bottle. Slip a wooden dowel through the holes. The dowel should be long enough to allow you a comfortable handle on both sides (see the illustration). Try it out. Does it spin if you hit it? If not, the holes might need to be to be enlarged. The person should have a seat and hold the bottle by the two handles in front of the dog at nose level. Let the dog watch his partner drop dry food into the top of the bottle. Encourage the dog to experiment with getting the food out by himself. Some dogs use their noses, others use their feet to spin the bottle.

A coachable moment

Teach a lesson on criteria selection and reinforcement—you might reinforce only using the paw or only using the nose. Be sure to control the spin of the bottle by squeezing it with the sides of your hands so the pay-off comes at the appropriate time.

Note: The bottle toy must be kept where the dog can't get it. He might tear it up and perhaps hurt himself on the sharp plastic or sticks. This is a cooperative toy, not a dog-only toy.

Ten Chances

Prerequisites and benefits

Dogs with a large repertoire of behaviors get to work at a distance from their partners. Partners will become aware of the importance of latency—an immediate response to a cue is beneficial in the Ten Chances game.

Set-up

Mark start and finish lines about 20 feet apart.

Description

The dog is left sitting on one line, his partner stands behind the other. She must get her dog from the start line to where she's standing on the finish line by giving him exactly ten different cues. Eleven cues won't count. Nine cues won't count. It has to be ten! An AGL is there to count cues and otherwise coach the participant to stay within the rules. The cues may be verbal or hand signals, but the cue must be given only once. Even if the dog doesn't respond properly or at all, that cue still counts in the ten allowed cues. Before the cue is given, the person announces what behavior is expected from her dog. This is important if you are playing competitively and have a scoring scheme in place. The tenth cue must bring at least one of the dog's feet over the finish line. A typical sequence might go like this: Dog is standing on the start line, owner says (1) Down, (2) Roll Over (3) Come, (4) Sit, (5) Stand, (6) Spin, (7) Stay, (8) Speak, (9) Sit Up, and (10) Target Touch.

Game variations

Play for fun and awareness of the dog's ability to respond to cues. If time permits, allow reruns. Alternatively, a time and/or point system for scoring could be put into place.

A coachable moment

I like to lead a brief discussion before this game, giving examples of possible strategies to help the dog succeed. You might ask the people if they have a plan for the possibility of the dog getting close to the finish line sooner than they had expected.

Tunnel of Love

Prerequisites and benefits

This is a game for dogs that are well-socialized and have experience complying with basic cues. It builds attention and recall skills for dogs while in proximity to other dogs.

Set-up

Mark two parallel lines with plenty of room (10 to 15 feet) between. The distance between lines depends on the stability of the dogs. The group is divided in two, each half on a line facing inward with their dogs in a sitting position facing the opposite line of dogs. Put place markers on the lines to be sure to keep appropriate distance, side to side, among those on the lines.

Description

Playing Tunnel of Love is good any time, but it helps perk up a dreary February as part of a Valentine's Day theme. The pair on the end walks through the tunnel. That pair then takes up a position on a marker at the far end of the tunnel. The dog then sits on a place mark on one side of the end of the tunnel. Next couple's turn. Periodically the GL might ask the lines to move up toward markers at the start, or you will be covering a lot of territory. Moving also gives the dogs a break from the sitting position.

Game variations

If all of the participants are advanced and dependable and you have lots of space between lines, the human partner can opt to leave her dog on a sit at the end of the tunnel, cross through alone, then call her dog. Work the dogs a little beforehand to make sure their social and training skills are up to this challenge.

Regardless of the version, the couple going through the tunnel can request the additional challenge of those on the sidelines tapping their feet slightly or singing quietly. This is a good distraction for their dogs too!

A coachable moment

This game gives the GL the opportunity to talk about personal space issues, consideration of others and ways to help dogs work on impulse control. You might mention that some dogs feel vulnerable in a down position and therefore it should be avoided.

Search Circle

Prerequisites and benefits
Builds fluency and encourages speed at retrieving for dogs that like to fetch.

Set-up
Place approximately 20 items of a variety of sizes, shapes and textures within a 20-foot circle. Set a timer for 20 seconds.

Description
"Ready? Begin." Dogs are sent individually to retrieve as many articles as they can in 20 seconds. Which couple or team retrieves the most articles?

Game variations
The nose knows: Encourage the dogs to use their noses by playing this in long grass. Use a seasonal theme by choosing particular music and the right selection of articles: Wrapped Christmas packages, tiny pumpkins, large toy Easter eggs, beach slippers or sand toys are some possibilities. Don't let anyone talk you into water balloons. Competitive: Put values on the items and count up the score.

A coachable moment
Share information: If there are people in the teams whose dogs don't retrieve, have the others say a few words about how they taught or encouraged their own dog to fetch. The GL can clarify any of that information and/or add to it. Then, for good will, play a different game just for the non-retrievers.

Christmas Stocking Relay

Prerequisites and benefits
Depending on the rules you establish, retrieving might be a prerequisite.

Set-up
Select teams. Prepare a tiny felt stocking on a red ribbon for the red team and a green ribbon for the green team. Each team has a starting point and a destination marker not too far away.

Description
In the basic game the ribbon is tied around the first dog's neck, allowing the stocking to dangle down in front of the dog's chest. One by one each couple walks on leash to their destination marker and back to the start where the stocking necklace is transferred to the next couple on his team. You might establish a tight-leash rule. A tight leash requires the dog to relinquish the stocking and go to the end of the line. When all dogs have had a turn, the game is over. First team finished is the winner.

Game variations
Competitive: Have lots of stockings. Instead of a relay, each dog leaves his stocking at the destination where an AGL tapes it up to a cardboard poster of a fireplace. When the time is up, count the stockings, and gather for a picture in front of the fireplace.

Retrieve: Change this game up a little. Instead of ribbon necklaces, give the green team a supply of green stockings, the red team a supply of red ones. Dogs need to get the stockings from the starting line to the fireplace where they're hung by an AGL. The dog can carry it in his mouth. A non-retriever can have the stocking tucked into his collar or harness. Maybe the dog will WEAR the stocking on a paw. Those little felt stockings don't fit dogs very well. I found that baby stretch socks are more apt to stay on.

Come Back, My Boomerang!

Prerequisites and benefits

Dogs with the confidence to work away from their partners will get experience being sent away to a target and back.

Set-up

Create a circle on the floor about five feet across. Mark a start line 10 feet away.

Description

The person "throws" the boomerang (sends her dog) to the circle. At least one paw needs to make it into the circle. The partner then calls her dog back close enough to be able to grasp his collar or harness.

Game variations

The dog can remain on a long line for this game. Increase the degree of difficulty by making the circle smaller and/or farther away.

A coachable moment

Chances are the dogs playing have not been taught a "Send away" or "Back up" cue. Have a pregame discussion about teaching those skills and perhaps doing it as homework. Also discuss various ways to get the dog to go to the circle, right now, with no time for proper training. Decide what options will be legal. Some ideas: Throw a toy, have an AGL show the dog a piece of food and then put it in the circle. Get your clicker out and shape the dog.

Decorate the Christmas Tree

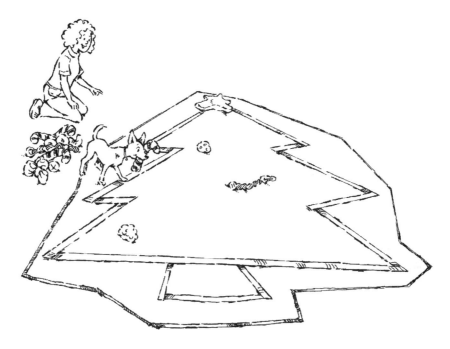

Prerequisites and benefits

This is for dogs experienced at retrieving and dogs that are target trained. Lateral thinking is required on the part of the humans. There's more than one way to decorate a tree (and still stay within the rules)!

Set-up

With green tape, make an outline of a large tree on the floor. 12 feet long is about right. Tape a foul line in a different color all around the tree, about 24 inches from the tree's perimeter. Prepare piles of garlands, non-breakable balls, large Styrofoam candy canes, big bows. Double check the ornaments for possible safety hazards. Find a star-shaped plastic dish. These are common in shops around Christmas time. Get one and put a little smear peanut butter in it. Place it at the top of the tree to create a diversion. Prepare a timer.

Description

The dog is asked to pick up an item from the pile of "ornaments" prepared beforehand, take the ornament to within the perimeter of the tree outline, drop it, and then return to his human partner, who has to stay outside of the foul line. The dog has 15 seconds to complete the task, during which holiday music is played. When the music goes off, that couple's time is up. Dogs take turns decorating the tree.

Game variations
To involve the target-trained dogs, place battery-operated push button lights in the tree. Dogs can turn on the Christmas tree lights. (See the Tic-Tac-Toe game on page 39 for details.)

Shoot the Basket

Prerequisites and benefits

A dog with some experience at taking cues at a distance will benefit from Shoot the Basket. He will have an opportunity to strengthen that skill. Humans will exercise their lateral thinking talents.

Set-up

A hoop is secured to the floor and a starting line is made about three feet away. A basketball-sized ball is placed on the floor at the starting line. You'll need a timing device.

Description

One by one, each dog has 15 seconds to get the ball into or through the hoop, while his partner stays behind the starting line. If they're not successful when the time is up, they simply go to the end of the line and try again.

Game variations

Play for points: One point if the ball touches any part of the hoop at least once, two for a ball rolling through the hoop to the other side, three for a ball landing in the hoop.

A coachable moment

A time-consuming version, but worth the ah-ha's it creates. My preference is to run Shoot the Basket as a lateral thinking game. Everyone watches as couples try one by one. If the first dog makes a basket by touching the ball with his nose, the rule for the next dog is "NOSE CANNOT BE USED." Perhaps the next dog is asked to roll over to propel the ball into the hoop: The rule for all subsequent plays is "NO NOSES OR ROLLING OVER." Putting these limitations in effect encourages new ideas to solve old problems. Albert Einstein: "The definition of insanity is doing the same thing over and over again and expecting different results."

Trash Collection

Prerequisites and benefits

The prerequisites depend on the behaviors chosen and listed on the exercise cards. These should be tailored to the skill level of the class. Mainly this activity is a chance to take a break and at the same time perform a basic scenting exercise.

Set-up

This game is played outside. Dog treats and exercise cards in envelopes are spread out in the yard ahead of time. Clearly define the search area so participants don't go too far afield.

Description

Everyone takes a walk in the fresh air while the dogs sniff for the goodies. The dogs eat the treats and their people collect the envelopes, saving them for later. When the group comes back together, each couple selects one exercise to show off to the group. Ask for a positive comment from the others about the performances.

Game variations

You might warm the dogs up to the idea of searching for the envelopes. People can allow their dog to sniff an envelope and immediately receive a treat from the envelope.

- **Competitive version:** Each couple performs all of their exercise cards, which have point values on them. Bringing back a plastic bag with poop in it gets extra points.

- **Laid-back version:** Skip the exercise cards, just find the envelopes, open and enjoy the goodies.

A coachable moment

Before you send them on the search, have a quick good citizen chat about being proactive at respecting personal space of others while on the course. Two dogs going for the same envelope? Someone has to turn away.

Jigsaw Puzzle Retrieve

Prerequisites and benefits

Some dogs are motivated to retrieve an item that has been thrown. Find out if the dogs will pick up a stationary article.

Set-up

Visit some garage sales or a Goodwill shop to find wooden preschool puzzles with extra-large pieces. Secure each puzzle piece in a recycled envelop or small paper bag to help the dogs get a good grasp and to prevent choking. All of those mismatched socks can be put to use: Loosely knot each piece into the toe of a sock. Divide the players into teams. You'll need start lines and destination markers. Pieces are placed in a pile or spread out at the destination marker for each team.

Description

One by one the dogs are asked to retrieve a puzzle piece and bring it back to their partners, who then assemble the puzzle. You might assign dogless spectators to each team as the assembly committee.

Game variations

On the back of each puzzle piece write a simple exercise already known to the group, for example "Sit for a count of three" or "Down for a count of five." The dog must perform that behavior before his piece can be fitted into the puzzle. If he can't do it on the first try, that piece goes back in the pile.

A coachable moment

Talk about the difference in motivation for some dogs to fetch a thrown object or an inanimate object.

What a Turkey!

Prerequisites and benefits

The dogs should have confidence enough to lie down briefly in what is likely a new setting for him. This is a good exercise for the introduction of and/or the use of clickers.

Set-up

Make a dog-sized roasting pan: Cut a large cardboard box so that the sides are only two to three inches high. Cover it with aluminum foil or silver-colored wrapping paper. To save valuable training time, create teams, each with their own pan. Perhaps a "big pan" team and a "small pan" team would be appropriate.

Description

Each dog is given a turn to lie down in the roasting pan.

Game variations

Competitive? Create a point schedule and play in teams: five points for a down, four points for a sit, three points for a brief stand, two points for a walk through, one point for a sniff or a drive-by. Minus five for a tight leash. To make the task even more challenging, add some large potatoes as distractions. Skip the onions. Ingesting onions can make a dog sick.

Want to have some fun? If the dog is acting silly, make a comment about him being a "ham" instead of a turkey. If he'd rather not sit or lie down, he can be a "standing rib roast."

A coachable moment

This game provides the opportunity to discuss and learn about the pros and cons of using lures. Explain how to shape the dog to step into the pan. Help participants select appropriate criteria for breaking down the exercise. Discuss the drawbacks of pulling or shoving the dog into the pan. Turn it into a shaping exercise using clickers.

Bobbing for Apples

Prerequisites and benefits
Basic retrieving skills are required. Dogs can work on retrieving fluency.

Set-up
A large tub or small child-sized swimming pool of water and a few small apples will be needed. Also provide a generous supply of towels.

Description
Dogs take turns retrieving an apple and giving it to their human partner. It can be so comical! Some dogs insist upon picking up the apples by the stem with their front teeth!

Game variations
Less messy version: No water, just apples.

Repurpose the apples: Send someone home with the apples and this recipe. Turn it into an actual "prize" by including a cheap rubber ice cube tray. To make dog apple treats, cut up four apples, discarding the core. Blend the pieces with one cup of nonfat plain yogurt. If the batter is too thick, add a bit of water to the mix. Pour into ice cube trays and freeze.

No-mess version of Bobbing for Apples: No water, no apples, just red rubber balls in a tub. Some greedy dogs will try to get several balls in their mouths at once!

Go fishing version: Stock the water-filled pool with Kongs, each having a tiny smear of something good inside. Dogs can take turns going fishing. Be sure to draw eyes, gills and scales on the Kongs.

Fortune cookie version: Prepare pieces of paper with typical "fortunes" and place one in each of several Kongs. Stock the dry tub with Kongs. Dogs take turns telling their person's fortune.

I Wonder What's in the Box?

Prerequisites and benefits

This game is good for dogs with at least a minimal ability to lie down and the inclination to stay if asked to do so. The dogs can work on self-control while their people interact with a box right in front of them.

Set-up

Wrap a few large boxes in pretty paper. Tie wide cloth ribbon around each, leaving ends long enough to tie into a bow. Divide the group into teams of three or four players each. Create a line on the floor for each team, where the couples will assemble side by side.

Description

Place a box, ribbon tied, within an arm's length in front of the first couple in each row. That dog is cued to lie down and stay while his partner unties and reties the bow and then pushes or passes the box to the next person, who does the same. The box must remain within an arm's length of each player. Repeat until the last couple in line has a turn.

Game variations

I've played the above in class every Christmas for years. If you are so inclined, you can turn this into a competition by asking the play to STOP if a dog on their team gets up. The dog must be settled back into a down before that team's play resumes. If you wanted to be even pickier, impose a three-second wait every time the dog extends his nose toward the gift box.

A coachable moment
It helps to remind the people that this is not a test, but a training opportunity. They could remind their dogs to stay, perhaps taking a few seconds to reinforce the position during their turn with the box.

Decathlon

Prerequisites and benefits

With 10 events from which to choose, Decathlon has something for everyone. The teams work together to determine how each couple can individually contribute to the success of their team as a whole. This is a team-building/good citizenship type of activity. It can also include a degree of lateral thinking.

Set-up

Divide the participants randomly into two or more teams. The behavior chosen for each of the ten events will dictate the props needed. You'll want to have some rousing stadium music on hand to play for the grand opening. Option: Have some fun by preparing an Olympic torch (a red dog toy on the end of a touch stick) and have someone run that around the arena before you start. A whiteboard and scoring cards will be needed if you play the competitive version.

Description

The Decathlon takes up a great deal of time. I feel it's worth the time due to the community spirit involved when the teams plan which members will participant in which events. The variations possible for the 10 basic events are endless. The players won't know the exact criteria for the basic exercise until just before that event begins. The same exact exercises are done for all teams. Prior to the start of the decathlon each team has a meeting and determines the strengths of each couple. Is there a gung ho retriever in the team? A really reliable recaller? Who is most apt to be rock solid on stays? The team leader then records which couples perform the events, making sure everyone on a team participates in the events as equally as possible. The decathlon begins, the GL announces the event and explains and demonstrates the way the exercise is to be performed. There is to be no practicing at all after the exercise is demonstrated. A couple from each team performs, then the GL presents the next event's exercise.

Here are some ideas for the GL.

Come event:

- Person sits in a chair with her back to the dog when she calls.
- Dog is held on leash by an AGL while his person goes out of sight before calling.

Leash event:

- Leash over person's shoulder. Figure 8 around cones. Does the leash slip?
- Heel backward on a tape line—at least five steps. Does the dog stay in position?

Sit event:

- Person puts a paper bag over her own head. Asks the dog to sit.
- Dog sits while nearby an AGL says "down" and "come."

Best trick event:

- Team's choice.

Target event:

- Person stays still, dog goes to a small mat six feet away.
- Dog's nose must touch a novel object.

Distance control event:

- Person sends dog around a cone six feet away.
- Dog is on a down-stay, partner walks ten paces and asks her dog to sit.

Obstacle event:

- Dog walks backward between two tables laid on end to form a chute.
- Dog walks over several hula hoops flat and overlapping without touching them.

Dancing event:

- Participant dances to 30 seconds of music of the GL's choice.

Retrieving event:

- Several rope toys loosely tied together.
- A package of chips.

Down event:

- Ball rolls by during the down.
- Dog must keep his head on the floor during down.

Game variations

The decathlon can be run as a competitive game. Announce scoring criteria. Some ideas might be: safety, creativity, minimized cues, and the dog's latency, speed and precision when executing the cue. Scoring is very tedious and subjective. You'll need to come up with some sort of point deduction plan for the judges. Recruit three impartial judges and give each ten pieces of cardstock numbered 1 to 10. After each contestant performs, the judges, without consulting with each other, hold up their scores. You could average the scores, but it's easier to just throw out the high and low scores and go with the middle number. Less prep work: Have the judges hold up fingers.

A coachable moment

After each contestant, have the other team make one positive comment about the performance. After all of the teams perform an event, the GL could conduct a training session about the exercise, focusing on it in two different ways:

- How you would train the behavior if you had plenty of time?
- What handling strategies could have been used to get the best performance on the spot?

Games for People Only

This section is to help people work on their coordination and skill as a trainer separately from working with their dog. Hey, it's only fair to improve the skills on both ends of the leash, right? I use variations of these exercises on a regular basis in my dog training and chicken training classes and workshops. Many of the games here are presented as clicker training exercises and assume you have already acquired the basics of clicker training. The exercises can be adapted and still be useful if your training doesn't involve using a marker. Most games are appropriate for introducing basic clicker skills to students who are inexperienced with clicker training. It's just a matter of a brief pregame lesson.

Here are a few of my favorite people-only mechanical skills games. Your search engine can help you find websites, computer programs and apps to practice your eye/hand coordination all by yourself.

Coasters

Prerequisites and benefits

This is a game for anyone with an understanding of the mechanical skills involved with using a clicker. I lead a game of Coasters at camps and workshops as a warm up in the morning or as a wake up for a mid-afternoon break. It's fast and has easy set-up, making it practical for one-hour sessions also. There are benefits to establishing strong and correct habits, through repetition, for the actions a trainer relies on regularly. In a way, this frees up the person's concentration for new information.

Set-up

Two trainers stand facing each other with a table between them. Three or four beverage coasters are spread out across the surface, a couple of inches apart, more if space allows. It's helpful to provide coasters that have a little ridge around the edge to prevent their contents from spilling out. Most dollar shops sell packages of plastic beverage coasters in a variety of colors. You'll need at least three different colors—four or five makes the game even more worthwhile. Position them upside down on the table so the lips can help keep the food in place. Keep in mind that some people can't distinguish between colors. If that's the case or if you can't find coasters in different colors, mark the coasters with big numbers or letters with a felt-tip pen. A good alternative if you can't find appropriate coasters is to use plastic snap-on pet food can covers. Find the cute versions with ears! I've been known to give them away to the players when the game is over.

Description

The players are wearing their treat pouches containing small, non-crumbly, non-sticky treats. Cut up jerky strips work well for this exercise. If treat pouches are not used, the food can be in a pocket or in a small container on the table. One person is designated Trainer and the other Coach. Roles will be reversed before the game is over to give both the full experience. Although you have lots of different colors in your set, start with only two. Make sure each couple has the same two colors as everyone else playing! A clicker is held in "home position" in one hand. The trainer herself determines what her home position will be. The clicker hand will remain there, still in the neutral position, throughout the training. The GL calls out a color. The sequence expected from the trainer is: listen for the color, keep still while clicking, then deliver the treat from its original location to the correct coaster. The click and delivery are sequential, not simultaneous. Next the GL calls out a different color. The GL varies the speed between calling the colors. The coach critiques the trainer after each session, concentrating on mentioning appropriate actions. Be specific: Rather than "good job," it might be more helpful to say "good job, clicker hand was still." You can also add points that could be improved: "Did you realize you were clicking and delivering the food at the same time?" After working together, you can probably shorten this feedback to "sequential." After two or three warm ups like this, the GL can ask for additional colors to be added to the two already on the table and conduct a few reps with all of the colors. Now it's time to switch roles. Go back to the original two colors to give the "new" trainer a chance to warm up and be critiqued before adding the additional colors.

Game variations

Make the exercise more challenging by giving both players a turn at experiencing one or more of these variations:

- The trainer switches her clicker to her non-dominant hand. This is just for experience. The trainer can decide which hand to use for the rest of the exercises.

- The coach will mix up the coasters between repetitions. As soon as the trainer delivers the treat, the coach reaches in and slides the coasters to a different position before the GL calls out the next color. Hopefully the coach will not dump out the food in the process. After several reps, the players switch roles. Repeat as you see fit.

- A greater skill challenge is to ask the trainer to turn her back to the table. When she hears the GL call out the color, she clicks, then turns to the table, delivers and turns away. The coach will have moved the coasters around while the trainer's back is turned. Repeat—but not too much. People get dizzy!

No competition, no scores, just friendly practice.

Don't Let Gravity Win

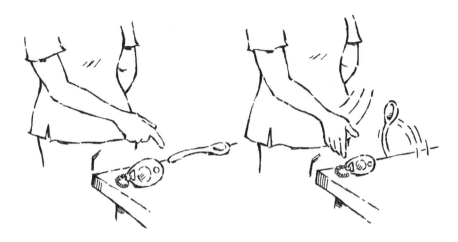

Prerequisites and benefits
An activity for everyone.

Set-up
I usually announce this challenge before a break so students can practice on their own time. Bring gift clickers for everyone. A clicker is placed on the edge of a table. A metal spoon is placed on the same edge, an inch away from the clicker.

Description
The trainer must use only one hand. The other is held behind her back during the exercise. The player nudges (not sling, or pick up and throw—just nudge!) the spoon so it falls to the floor. With the same hand, the trainer immediately picks up the clicker and clicks. If the click sounds before the sound of the spoon hitting the floor, she beats gravity. This works best if the table is on a hard floor so you can hear the spoon when it hits. The first student to show success after the break gets a round of applause from the others—and gets to keep the clicker. Usually everyone wants to meet the challenge, and they do! In any case, everyone gets a new clicker!

Game variations
Don't Let Gravity Win is a good lead-in for participants making beaded tails for their clickers. See next page.

Beaded Clicker Tails
(aka TAGulators)

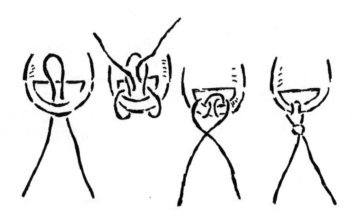

Prerequisites and benefits

This is a "camp craft" for everyone. A clicker with a tail is more easily found in the bottom of your purse or in the back of your drawer. Add to that benefit by using glow-in the dark beads! The tail is a series of beads on a string. One helpful use of the clicker tail: The tail can be used to help the GL keep track of turns. Sometimes I ask two teams to take two turns each, alternating. With all the commotion, I want to make sure I don't forget that last, fourth turn. To keep track, I slide beads as each team finishes so no one misses a turn.

Set-up/supplies needed for each participant:

- An 18-20 inch length of cord. Must be: 2mm rattail satin to fit the beads properly.
- Four beads. Must be "pony beads," which have the proper-sized opening.
- Optional: Tiny carabiner or tiny snap (like on leashes) or a small split ring.
- Optional: Some craft glue.

All of the above can be found in the craft section of a department store.

Description/instructions:

- Double the string in half.
- Push the loop end of the doubled string halfway through the clicker's opening.
- Pull the clicker half way down the two strings.
- Put the two string tails into the loop of the string and pull.

- You now have a clicker secured on one end and two strings dangling from it.
- Thread one bead onto one string, pull it half way down.
- Grab the empty tail, poke the end through the same bead, only from the opposite side.
- You now have an X with a bead in the middle.
- Pull the bead down to the clicker.
- Repeat with the differently colored bead.
- Makes no difference which string goes first.
- Do it again two more times until you have four beads in alternating colors.
- Where you tie the knot depends on how far you want to slide the beads.
- I find a little less than an inch left for sliding beads is about right.
- Tie a "stopper" knot tight. Any knot will do. I use an overhand knot.
- You can tie the remaining tails in a knot around the carabiner, snap or ring.
- Leftover string can be made into a bow.
- Try it out!
- If you like the spacing, squeeze a dab of glue on all knots and allow to dry.

You can use the carabiner to attach the clicker to your bait pouch, belt loop or zipper pull so it's always within easy grasp.

Note: Originally known as TAGulators, I was taught how to make these when I hosted my first TAGteach workshop years and years ago. Search the internet for more about TAG (Teaching with Acoustical Guidance) and TAGulators. Excuse me, TAG people, for adapting your idea in form and function for a different use.

Bop It!

Prerequisites and benefits

Bop It is a game for everyone. It works on coordination, reaction time and teamwork.

Set-up/description

This plastic toy is available at most department stores or online. There are several versions of it. I like the original Bop It as shown in the illustration. When you activate the toy, the little man inside tells you what to do with the knobs and handles sticking out of the main body of the toy. You'll hear "Pull It," Twist It" and the like. The longer you play, the faster the little man is at making his requests. If you happen to be too slow for his approval, he'll shout out an insult and the game is over for you. That's not very positive, is it? You can talk about how it feels to be ridiculed for not measuring up to someone else's expectations. The best part of the game is when the little man inside tells you to "Pass It." You are off the hook for playing, but you need to efficiently hand the toy over to the next person on your team. That person needs to focus quickly because the little man does not let up on his demands during a pass.

You might need to split the group, each with their own toy, to reduce standing-around time. Keep the teams well apart, because this game can become exciting and noisy. In their enthusiasm, the players can drown out the instructions from the little man, which increases your chance for another insult.

A coachable moment

Seriously speaking, teaching how to play Bop It allows you to talk about breaking the task down, teaching it bit by bit. Passing is the weak link. People can get into trouble easily while passing, so lead a discussion about passing strategies. Before you start the game, have a session with the GL calling out the various instructions the little man inside will be giving you. Individuals can practice what to do when they hear you say "Pull It" for example. Then mix in other actions. Talk about how teams, by planning together, can optimize their chance for success, especially when passing the toy. I've been known to purchase little keychain versions of Bop It for prizes.

No, I do not own stock in the company. They should pay me, though. I've introduced this toy at workshops all over the world.

Round Robin

Prerequisites and benefits

Some trainers will toss the dog's treat away to a predetermined location rather than feed directly to his mouth. For some training applications, this positions the dog optimally for the next rep. It can be a challenge to get the food exactly where you want it, especially if the food is not aerodynamically correct. Round Robin helps with aim and coordination. It is assumed that the players know the basics of using a clicker. If not, conduct a brief pregame lesson.

Set-up

You'll need a clicker and a small plastic bag of popcorn for each player. Form a circle with chairs facing inward. Place a small bowl on the floor in the middle of the circle, at least six feet from the chairs.

Description

Players sit in chairs and remain there throughout the exercise. One by one they take turns tossing a piece of popcorn into the bowl. Hitting the target is difficult, and the popcorn often bounces out of the bowl, but they can make adjustments with each subsequent turn and become more and more successful. (When the game is over, someone can take the popcorn to a park and feed the squirrels!)

Game variation

Skip the clicker and have the players work with the primary reinforcer only.

A coachable moment

"If at first you don't succeed, try, try again." – William Edward Hickson

Odd or Even?

Prerequisites and benefits

This is another simple game of eye/hand coordination for people who have basic mechanical skill with clicker training.

Set up

Two trainers stand facing each other with a table between them. They are each holding a clicker in their chosen home position. Each table has one regular board-game-sized die.

Description

Ask for a volunteer to help you demonstrate the game. You portray the "even" player and the volunteer is the "odd" player. Even always goes first. To begin the game, the even player rolls the die onto the table. If it turns up an odd number, the odd player clicks, picks it up and rolls it again. If an even number turns up, the even player clicks, picks up the die and rolls again. This can be a fast-moving game. Let the people play for about 30 seconds and call "time" for them to stop. Play a couple of 30-second rounds, then ask the players to exchange roles. The odd person is now even and vice versa! This can be a difficult transition for the players. I lighten up the experience by saying something like, "It's great to make mistakes on a piece of plastic instead of our dogs."

Game variations

For a mathematical challenge, use two dice. Skip the clicker and have players use a verbal marker. Don't use a marker at all and just go for the grab and toss.

A coachable moment

Play a couple more rounds. Point out that Odd or Even is a useful exercise because trainers often have to revise or change their minds quickly about what to reinforce when shaping their dog's behavior.

Rapidly Changing Criteria

Prerequisites and benefits

This game provides practice defining, identifying and marking rapidly changing criteria. It is assumed that the players have the basics of the mechanical skills involving clicker training.

Set-up

Divide a few decks of playing cards into piles of red and black cards. You might want to do away with the Jokers as they sometimes confuse the players. Divide the cards into mini-decks of around 15 to 20 cards, about half red and half black in each mini deck. Shuffle. Two players stand face to face with a table between them. One is the trainer and has a clicker held in home (neutral) position of the trainer's choice. The other is the dealer.

Description

Demonstrate this game ahead of time, with you playing the dealer. The dealer holds the deck, number sides down. The dealer drops the cards, one by one, on the table so that the plain back side of the card is up. The trainer's task is to click at the instant the card hits the table, not before, not after. The dealer should make it a point to be somewhat slow at dropping the cards at first until the trainer is warmed up. Play stops when the last card at every table is dealt. Shuffle the cards. This time the dealer drops the cards face side up. Before the play starts, the GL declares red or black. If red is declared, only red cards should be marked. The black cards are ignored. The trainer's task is now two-fold: the trainer still needs to click exactly when the card hits the table, but now has the added criterion of only clicking the red cards. Switch roles and play again.

Game variations

A more challenging version is for the GL to change which color is to be marked a couple of times while the deck is still in play. Perhaps the game starts with red. During the play the GL will call out "black, now mark black." In a few seconds the GL might call out "red, now mark red." If you want to be tricky, the GL can call out "Face cards only, mark any color face card." Another way to keep the players sharp is to call out the same color twice in a row. For example if the players are marking black, call out "Black, now mark black." Some people automatically change to the other color. They weren't listening. Oops!

A coachable moment

Please note that no primary reinforcement is included in this drill. We are concentrating on the clicker skill only this time. Don't forget to switch dealers with trainers so that each participant has equal time at each game version. Ask the group if anyone made an error. Tell them it's better to make mistakes with pieces of paper rather than with people and dogs.

Quick Draw

Prerequisites and benefits

Rate of reinforcement for training is an important factor to consider in your lesson plans. Speed is one attribute for delivering an appropriately high rate of reinforcement. This game stresses speed.

Set-up

Two human players stand facing each other with a table between them. They are each holding a clicker in their chosen home position. Each has a supply of treats in their pouches. There is a small bowl on the table in front of each trainer.

Description

When the AGL calls "Begin," players click in home position and deposit the reinforcer into their bowl, repeatedly until the AGL calls "Time." The duration of the session is 30 seconds. How many pieces of food are in the bowl? Since rate of reinforcement is almost always referred to as "per minute," double that number and mark down the total. Empty the bowl. Round two. Can the players increase by at least one reinforcement? Can they do so without fumbling with their treat pouches? Are they still able to keep their hand in home position? Are they really clicking and THEN moving their hand toward the pouch for the treat? Remember, it's click, then treat, two consecutive motions, not click and treat at the same time.

Game variations

Have the students fill out a rate of reinforcement graph. A simple version appears on page 149.

A coachable moment

It's counter-productive to have folks work with a clicker if they don't understand the mechanics of marking the appropriate criteria and delivering the reinforcer. Have a quick pregame lesson on the points mentioned above if you suspect this weakness.

Silence is Golden: a Table Top Shaping Exercise

Prerequisites and benefits

Prerequistes—zero. Benefits—too numerous to mention.

Set-up

Two participants sit face to face with a table between them. One is the learner, one is the trainer. They need one shaping kit between them. You'll need a timing device. Silence Is Golden is a mechanical skills game for humans only. It is my own knock-off of an interactive exercise created in the 1960s by the Brelands. Much later a different version was made popular by Karen Pryor. Since then, there have been many adaptations of this exercise by trainers all over the world. Here's the version I play. I call it "Silence Is Golden" because I like to show the value of having the clicker do the talking. If your players are new to clicker training, be sure to coach the basics as you go along with Silence Is Golden. The object of the game is not to get the learner to actually perform the task. Rather, I like to stress this concept: "The importance is not in the destination, it's in the journey."

The shaping kit

Five small objects are needed: The toy section of a department store has bags of little toys like plastic animals, from which you can choose. Any small item that the learner can manipulate will be fine: dice, dominos, Legos, coins, paper clips, poker chips.

Two preprinted behavior cards: I want behaviors that are simple, non-invasive and have a reasonable goal for the learner. An example might be: "Place the coin on top of the paper clip." This task would be too complex for this version of the game: "Place the coin on top of the paper clip, move them both to the edge of the table, then take the coin off the clip and place it back on the table." To keep the behaviors simple, I create them and print them out ahead of time on cards or slips of paper rather than allow the trainer to come up with their own behaviors.

15 to 20 "treats": Dry beans or pieces of dog kibble, or even small buttons are easily handled and can represent the training treats.

Two index cards: The trainer piles the treats on one index card on the table in front of her representing a treat pouch. The learner has the other index card on the table in front of him, which represents his "stomach."

A clicker: You'll only need one for both players

Description

Simple shaping tasks will be assigned. The participants take turns being the trainer and the learner. Each pair has a shaping kit—the same set of playing pieces in a plastic bag. The game is a series of three one-minute sessions done simultaneously by the entire group, sitting in pairs, each with a table between them (after an initial demo by the GL). Stress that we are doing this exercise to help elicit later conversation about what the learner might be learning, which is often different from what the trainer actually conveys or thinks she conveys. "Silence Is Golden." I enforce silence during the game because often comments that players blurt out to each other are priceless—a top notch ah-ha learning experience I'd like them to share with the ENTIRE group. I lead the discussion systematically between each training session.

The designated trainer chooses, at random, one of the preprinted behaviors provided in the kit to teach the learner across the table. (No peeking at the other paper.) The trainer takes a few minutes, apart from the learner, to get a shaping plan in mind. When the timer starts the first session, the learner begins to investigate the five items placed on the table. The learner is restricted to using only one hand, the same hand, throughout the entire game, putting the other in his lap. This makes the learner more dog-like. This makes it easier for the trainer to reset between reps. When the learner hears the click, he takes the treat offered to him by the trainer (with his one hand) and places it on his stomach marker. We keep track of rate of reinforcement and how criteria selection influences it. For the tasks I create, the minimum acceptable rate of reinforcement is 10 to 15 per minute. Count the number of treats in the stomach at the end of each session. Can the criteria be lowered during the next session to keep the rate of reinforcement higher? You might have each table record the data on a rate of reinforcement graph. A sample appears on page 149.

Each one-minute session can end in one of three ways: (1) When the timer announces session over. Remind players to keep quiet, and be prepared to discuss thoughts when the whole class can listen in. It's important not to let the learner know yet what the behavior is. He has two more sessions to go; (2) When the learner appears to have done the task ONCE as it's written on the card. The trainer shouldn't keep going to make sure. For this game, stop as soon as the action looks like what was written on the paper. The trainer congratulates the learner and refrains from saying anything more; and (3) Any time the trainer or learner appears to be overly confused or stressed, the trainer of the team can call the end of the session.

A coachable moment (or many moments!)

No one is expected to actually be successful at the behavior, although some will. More important is the ability to talk, when all three sessions are over, about what took place. Often exploring why the goal was not attained is the better lesson anyway! Lessening the focus on the goal reduces stress on the players. Working in short sessions with a specific ending time also cuts down on what I have come to consider a waste of time with unguided, ineffective shaping taking place during the exercise. Between and after sessions we talk about task analysis, identifying criteria, marking clearly defined criteria and efficient delivery of reinforcement, resetting between repetitions if necessary to repeat the task, superstitious behavior, and lots of other details. Perhaps one table's behavior involved only two of the five items. Point that out if the trainer failed to "clean up" his training area of these irrelevant distractions. You decide what is important to you and include those issues between sessions. Be sure to eventually give the participants a chance to talk to each other and to discuss how the session might have gone differently. It's especially important for the trainer to find out what the learner was "thinking"—something you can't ask your dog. Here's an example: The task was to put the coin on the paper clip. The behavior card didn't say heads up. The learner was reinforced for placing it heads up and now believes that is an important part of the behavior. Maybe the behavior was to move the blue chip to the edge of the table. He did it the first few times, not realizing the color was important. Next time he moves the yellow chip to the edge of the table. Bad dog! You know better than that! This is what could be happening when your dog suddenly seems to be refusing to respond appropriately. He never really understood the criteria. I wish dogs could talk.

Trials

	1	2	3	4	5	6	7	8	9	10
Criteria										
30										
29										
28										
27										
26										
25										
24										
23										
22										
21										
20										
19										
18										
17										
16										
15										
14										
13										
12										
11										
10										
9										
8										
7										
6										
5										
4										
3										
2										
1										

Number of Click and Deliveries per Minute

About the Author

Terry Ryan and her husband, Bill, live on the Olympic Peninsula in Washington State. They raised their daughter and son with a wide variety of animals including, of course, dogs! Terry was a stay-at-home mom for several years. She did some undergraduate study in psychology at Washington State University and was the Program Coordinator for the Dean of the College of Veterinary Medicine there from 1981 until 1994. The programs involved the study of the human-animal bond and implementation of animal-assisted activity/therapy programs.

Terry has been a dog trainer and/or instructor continually since the late 1960's. Early on she founded *Legacy Canine Behavior & Training, Inc.,* an organization specializing in non-coercive training methods for people and their dogs.

Terry trained her own dogs for various performance events including tracking and obedience. She was an AKC obedience trial judge for years. From the summer of 1997 to 2002, she worked with others to teach six-day behavior courses at the American Wildlife Foundation, using imprinted wolves as the study subjects. Terry has had long-term contracts in several countries to create curricula and teach national dog training and instructor training programs.

For many years the Ryans operated a large training facility and managed staff teaching a variety of training specialties. Puppy classes were held twice a week, continually, every week of the year. The place was designed and built especially for training and included features such as a private dog park for their clients, an extensive library, behavior consultation offices and various training and agility fields. To satisfy one of Terry's passions, the campus doubled as a state-of-the-art chicken training facility.

Numerous times a year Terry teaches the Karen Pryor Academy in the USA and abroad. Through Legacy, she maintains a vigorous national and international workshop and seminar schedule. Her most popular workshops include *Legacy's Chicken Training Camps,* her instructor's course, *Coaching People to Train Their Dogs,* her *Training Games Workshops* and one on behavior modification entitled *Tools for Change: From Possibility to Probability–the Positive Way!*

Terry has maintained membership and held various offices in local, national and international organizations. She's served on various advisory boards. She has written several books and booklets published in several languages about training and instruction including the textbook, *Coaching People to Train Their Dogs* and *The Toolbox for Building a Great Family Dog.* Keep in touch with what Terry is up to at www.legacy.com.

Also available from Dogwise Publishing

Go to www.dogwise.com for more books and ebooks.

The Toolbox for Building a Great Family Dog

Terry Ryan

Make dog training a pleasure with these fun and positive methods. With clear explanations for how a dog thinks, how to read canine body language and moving on to simple training exercises, you will soon have a "great family dog."

> *"The Toolbox for Building a Great Family Dog* will be an invaluable resource for guardians of companion dogs. Terry has a rare skill for compelling writing, a pleasure to read. She backs this up with practical solutions for basic training as well as taking it to the next level and resolving common problem behaviors. "

James O'Heare, CABC, PABC, author of *Changing Problem Behavior, Empowerment Training*

How to Run a Dog Business. Putting Your Career Where Your Heart Is, 2nd Ed

Veronica Boutelle

The demand for skilled dog trainers, dog walkers, pet sitters and dog daycare and boarding operators has never been greater. And you'll need more than dog expertise to succeed—you'll need business savvy too. Let this book be your roadmap.

> "Invaluable practicalities, counsel, structure, and support."

Jean Donaldson, author of *Culture Clash* and Director of The Academy for Dog Trainers

> "An extraordinarily valuable book. Veronica gives great advice to trainers and would-be trainers. My advice is to read this book!"

Trish King, author of *Parenting Your Dog* and Director of Canine Behavior Associates

Play with Your Dog

Pat Miller, CPDT, CDBC

Play is essential to the well-being of your dog and for developing sound social relationships between dogs and dogs and dogs and humans. Learn how to use play to socialize, stimulate and enjoy your best friend.

"This extremely user-friendly book will inspire and instruct anybody seeking to strengthen their relationship with dogs through play. It's for every dog person, from the novice pet owner to the professional trainer and opens up a new world of joyful communication. Play is one of the most significant tools in the trainers' toolbox. Now go out and play!"

Leslie McDevitt, MLA, CDBC, CPDT, author of *Control Unleashed*

Fetch More Dollars For Your Dog Training Business

John D. Visconti, CPDT-KA

At last, sales coaching for dog trainers! Meet your own personal sales coach, author John Visconti. Dog trainers generally don't think of themselves as salespeople—many in fact recoil at the thought! However, when you define selling as the process of communicating the benefits that your services can provide to owners and their dogs, you realize that you must be an effective salesperson to have a successful business. John takes the mystery and fear out of the selling process in this book which belongs in the toolbox of every professional dog trainer.

"I love this book. I really like the style—well written, catchy and always straight to the point. At long last, an approach that focuses on the people-motivating aspects of the business of pet dog training. It doesn't matter how good you are at training dogs, if you lack sales savvy and people skills for promotion, few dogs will benefit from your experience and expertise."

Dr. Ian Dunbar, Founder of The Association of Professional Dog Trainers.

Mind Games for Dogs
Dogwise Solutions

Sarah Whitehead

Boredom can lead to problems in dogs. By challenging your dog's mind with easy brain games, behavior improves and the fun begins! Learn indoor and outdoor games that let her hunt for her food, read signs and escape from a maze.

Also available in packs of 25 and 50.

Human Half of Dog Training. Collaborating with Clients to Get Results

Risë VanFleet, PhD, CDBC

Dog trainers don't really train dogs—they train people to train their dogs. Learn how to empathize with clients, overcome common objections and work with families to get the best results for the dog. From a PhD Psychologist-turned-dog-trainer.

"*The Human Half of Dog Training* is a practical and theoretical book that fills a much-needed hole in the dog training literature. Risë's background in working with humans, combined with her skills as a dog trainer, give her a unique perspective on how to get our clients on board. If you've ever been frustrated by your clients' resistance or lack of follow-through, this book is for you!"

Grisha Stewart, MA, CPDT-KA, KPACTP, author of *Behavior Adjustment Training*

Dogwise.com is your source for quality books, ebooks, DVDs, training tools and treats.

We've been selling to the dog fancier for more than 25 years and we carefully screen our products for quality information, safety, durability and FUN! You'll find something for every level of dog enthusiast on our website www.dogwise.com or drop by our store in Wenatchee, Washington.

Made in the USA
Columbia, SC
10 January 2020